hay fever

hay fever

HOW CHASING A DREAM
ON A VERMONT FARM
CHANGED MY LIFE

ANGELA MILLER

WITH RALPH GARDNER JR.

WILEY

JOHN WILEY & SONS, INC.

Copyright © 2010 by Angela Miller and Ralph Gardner Jr. All rights reserved
Jacket photography: front cover, farm © Francesco Tonelli; front cover, city
© iStockphoto/Xaviarnau; back cover, farm © Chris Gray
Interior photography: title page, barn © Chris Gray;
chapter openers, goat, and recipes opener, cheese © Laura Brown
Published by John Wiley & Sons, Inc., Hoboken, New Jersey
Published simultaneously in Canada

Interior design by Debbie Glasserman
Illustrations by Rebecca Scherm

LIBRARY OF CONGRESS CATALOGING-IN-PUBLICATION DATA
Miller, Angela, 1947-
Hay fever : how chasing a dream on a Vermont farm changed my life / Angela Miller
with Ralph Gardner Jr.
p. cm.
Includes index.
ISBN 978-0-470-39833-3 (cloth)
1. Farm life—Vermont. 2. Country life—Vermont. I. Gardner, Ralph, 1953- II. Title.
S521.5.V5M55 2010
630.92—dc22
[B]
2009033735

Printed in the United States of America
10 9 8 7 6 5 4 3 2 1

contents

CONTENTS

from where i stand

ON A JUNE MORNING IN 2009, I RAN OVER TO THE BARN
parking lot to greet the cheese inspector, Greg Lockwood. After six
years of monthly visits, he's more than a little familiar with the
history of our goat farm and its challenges. After chatting a few
minutes, I couldn't contain my pride and blurted out, "For the
first time, I think I have it under control."

Greg just shook his head.

"It's a farm," he said, chewing his words in a typical Vermont
fashion. "Just when you think you've got it down, all hell will
break loose and you'll find out just how much you don't know and
how little control you actually have."

He's right about that. A cheese farmer is at the total mercy of nature—as well as unexpected natural disasters. Healthy goats can suddenly come down with mastitis infections, anemia, bloat, pinkeye, and an array of baffling diseases. Cheese may develop molds you weren't aware grew on this planet. Employees you'd thought were devoted can quit at a moment's notice. The well can run dry, the grain can be tainted, and the cheeses can become ammoniated and virtually worthless to anyone but the pigs.

But this year is an oasis of calm compared to the upheaval of 2008, which I write about in *Hay Fever*. The entire agricultural year—from kidding in April through breeding season in November—was a tumultuous time on Consider Bardwell Farm, though I didn't anticipate that when I set out to write this book. At that point, I simply knew we were trying to double cheese production and turn a profit, or at least break even. And we seemed to be heading in the right direction: We were developing a first-class team of cheese makers, winning awards, and signing up great distributors. But then the economy tanked and with it the public's eagerness to splurge on artisanal cheese, no matter how delicious and well crafted.

Add to those challenges the insanity of my own career—or should I say careers. Most people who come to farming in middle age are intent on making it their second career and have the savvy to retire from their first, hopefully with a handsome little nest egg. Not me. I decided I could do both: run a literary agency in New York City, my vocation for the last twenty-five years, and manage a farm, with which I had zero experience.

I'd never give up the publishing business, and not just because I need the income to help support the farm. I truly enjoy working with my authors—even the difficult ones; they are often the most inspired, creative, and passionate. I love nurturing their careers and developing relationships that often transcend business to become genuine friendships.

I would also never want to escape the city completely. In fact, I live in a crazy cycle—switching between city girl and country girl modes every few days. As much as I love the farm, the goats, and the people who work with me, it also feels great to know I can flee once a week and with it the decisions and the relentless responsibilities. The farm and the landscape are lovely, but there's just so much natural beauty you can take before you long for the intensity of an energized city like New York—the staccato sounds of traffic or seeing a thousand unknown faces on any given day that ignite the imagination. Then again, the frenetic pace of the city makes returning to Vermont all the more precious and also makes me realize it's here in the country, among my goats and feasting on our very own handmade cheeses, where I've found my place. My heart and mind have room for both city and country life, and my time spent in either one helps me better appreciate the other.

But sometimes the insanity of this bipolar existence overwhelms me. On a Thursday night, I may share an exquisite meal with a big name in the food world at the latest restaurant. The next morning, it would not be unusual for me to find myself hauling fifty-pound bales of hay at 5 A.M. to the goats in the barn when it's ten degrees outside, and it occurs to me that I have workers' compensation insurance for everybody on the farm except me. I pause not to appreciate Vermont's breathtaking landscape, but to catalog my aches and pains and feel like a damn fool. Then I remind myself to keep moving because I have to negotiate an author contract and order farm supplies later that morning.

For those who fantasize about the simple life on a farm and think it might be fun to raise goats and make cheese, consider this book a cautionary tale: You should know about the bruises from wrestling ravenous goats, shoes caked with manure, feet frozen and aching from standing on cold concrete all day, and mountains of invoices on Monday mornings and deciding which to pay and which to postpone. You may suffer through soaring expenses, more than occasional spasms of self-doubt, and many forms of medical and mechanical disasters.

Nevertheless, you might be armed with the proper combination of drive, idealism, and enabling delusions, like I was, to get you through. After all, we've been at it six years and came through the "Great Recession" of 2008 alive and even stronger. This year, we stand poised—and I emphasize the tentative nature of the word *poised*—to make a little money. People love our cheese, it's selling well, it's winning even bigger prizes, and the operation has never run more smoothly.

People might say that there are simpler, more straightforward ways to run not only a farm, but a life. Unfortunately, this all-engines-running mode is the only way I know. I'm acutely aware that I'm on the wrong side of sixty, and though many people my age are winding down, I am energized by the pleasure that comes with waking up each morning to face a world that's no less novel than it was in my teens and twenties. For that, I feel extraordinarily grateful. And I owe that to the farm and all of the people there who have stuck with me through feast and famine.

ANGELA MILLER

CONSIDER BARDWELL FARM

MARCH 2010

ONE

green mountain high

I WAS HAVING LUNCH WITH ONE OF MY AUTHORS AT SAN Domenico, an upscale Italian restaurant until recently on Central Park South in Manhattan, one wintry day in 2004 when the farm number appeared on my cell phone. That wasn't good. With a few exceptions, I try to keep my clients in the dark about my other life as a farmer. During my years as a literary agent, I've discovered that clients need your full attention during a meeting, and I've developed a professional rule that my personal business should never intrude on a relationship with a client. Some writers are particularly sensitive about needing center stage; I can't say I blame them, given the years of blood, sweat, and tears they put into a book that could easily vanish without a trace. Each author wants to be confident that you're there for him or her, and in the best of all possible worlds, he or she would be your only client. You would devote yourself 24/7 to him or her and have no spouse, no friends, and no vacations to get in the way, let alone a three hundred–acre farm in Vermont with a hundred needy goats and a labor-intensive cheese-making operation. I have no doubt that if many authors knew about my other life, some would fire me. Some already have.

On a one-to-ten scale of insecure authors, my lunch partner ranked near the top. There have been occasions when her husband called because she was having a panic attack about her career—which is doing quite nicely, actually—and he needed my help calming her down. So when my cell phone signaled a call during our lunch, I looked down discreetly, saw it was from the farm, and froze. I remained outwardly calm, but my mind was racing. I was afraid that there was some farm calamity: Maybe a goat was sick or had even died. Perhaps the milking equipment had broken down; it wouldn't be the first time.

"It's Samantha, my daughter," I lied. (Everyone understands taking calls from offspring.) I ran outside into the December sleet to take the call.

It was my twenty-two-year-old farmhand, Abby Rawlings, who was in tears. She confessed that she had forgotten to close the door to the chicken coop after cleaning it out. In her absence, a neighbor's dog dropped by and took advantage of the opportunity, killing every single chicken. Abby was inconsolable. "Abby," I tried to reassure her, "It's okay. You didn't do anything wrong. We'll get new chickens." Luckily, we were in the goat cheese business, not the egg business. (And she didn't tell me that she'd actually gone up into the haymow with her boyfriend to have the proverbial roll in the hay, which our handyman revealed to me a year later, with an accompanying belly laugh.)

Chickens were the least of my worries at that moment. I was acutely aware that eight minutes had passed since I'd abandoned my client, leaving her to brood about her career over veal piccata. Knowing her, I imagined she was already searching the Internet on her BlackBerry for a new agent. I rushed back inside, my silk Armani jacket soaking wet. I told her that my daughter had this or that problem—dismissing the poor child in a single sentence— and we got back to our discussion about what I was doing to sell foreign rights to her book.

And that, in a nutshell, is my dual-track life.

There are some people—for want of a better word, let's call them *normal*—who decide to switch careers when they hit their forties or fifties. They want to spend more time with their kids or be closer to nature. They suspect that there's more to life than riding the crowded subway to work, working for an impersonal corporation, and getting a measly two weeks of vacation per year. They might have saved a little money, or better, a lot of money. Then, perhaps inspired by books such as Michael Pollan's *The Omnivore's Dilemma*, they sell the apartment, move to an idyllic state like Vermont, and start to milk cows, raise pigs, or grow organic lettuce.

I never dreamed of leaving book publishing, and that was a

darn good thing. Besides loving books and enjoying my relationships with my authors, I couldn't afford the life of a farmer. There was never any doubt that I needed the income from my job as partner in The Miller Literary Agency, as well as the help of my husband, Rust, who is an architect. There's an old joke that says the best way to be worth a million bucks as a farmer is to start with two million. They're talking about me.

I'm proud of where we are now: making fifty thousand pounds of cheese annually, winning prizes, selling at a dozen farmers' markets, and being on the cheese cart at some of the finest restaurants in the country, such as Jean Georges, Daniel, Blue Hill at Stone Barns, and the French Laundry. But getting to that point has cost hundreds of thousands of dollars in equipment, salaries, marketing, and distribution—not to mention the cost of developing, feeding, and caring for a healthy herd of dairy goats.

And that doesn't include the thousands of hours of sweat equity my husband, Rust, and I have devoted to the enterprise over the last eight years, starting when we bought the farm in 2001 as our refuge from the real world, acquiring a few goats in 2003 to make cheese, making some more cheese and starting to develop delusions of grandeur, hiring a professional cheese maker in 2004 who persuaded some of the country's best restaurants to include our farm's bounty on their cheese plates, getting an even more ambitious cheese maker in 2007 and ramping up production, and winning awards in 2008 that made us think even bigger. The only thing we haven't done so far—and it's not insignificant— is turn a profit.

That's part of the reason I work in the city on Tuesday, Wednesday, and Thursday, wearing my Marc Jacobs suit and Jimmy Choo mules: I meet with authors and editors, have the occasional social dinner, and more often than not, eat takeout. Then on Thursday afternoon, I make the transition to my other world. In an often futile effort to beat rush-hour traffic, I get in my secondhand Audi station wagon no later than 4 P.M. (on a good day) and head out of Manhattan along the West Side Highway, with the majestic Hudson River on my left, then continue up the Taconic State Parkway. I'll get out my phone list, hit the speaker-phone button, and start returning calls—about the only time I can do so in a reasonably relaxed environment.

It might seem strange that a "reasonably relaxed environment" is one where I'm operating a moving vehicle on a packed New York highway, but that's the only time I have to myself. The drive gives me time to think and make my voluminous "to-do" lists (though only in my head; I try to keep my hands on the wheel). This is also my moment to decompress and listen to National Public Radio. I'll also receive calls from Sharon Bowers and Jennifer Griffin, my partners in the Miller Literary Agency, who know that this is the best time to talk. Without their sharp management skills and reliability, I couldn't pull off my dual existence.

The Taconic is a beautiful, one-hundred-five-mile linear parkway that snakes northward from Westchester County most of the way to Albany. It's perhaps the only route out of Manhattan that isn't plagued by constant traffic jams—and for good reason. Many people are terrified of the Taconic. Dating back to the 1920s, the parkway has sharp curves and claustrophobic towering rock walls. There's no margin for error, especially in the rain or snow.

But there's something therapeutic, even Zen-like, about it. If you're focused on staying alive, you tend to think less about your weight or being poor (my two obsessions—oh, and now aging). And once I get off the Taconic and hit the back roads of upstate New York, the landscape is even less populated and more serene. The area between Manhattan and Albany has become increasingly suburban, but New York City's sphere of influence wanes the further north you go. After exiting the Taconic, my drive to Consider Bardwell Farm takes me another eighty miles, just across the border into western Vermont. As I drive up Route 22— the road that goes all the way to Salem, New York, only eight miles from the farm in West Pawlet—I like to imagine that this stretch of land looks much the way it did fifty years ago: sparsely settled, hardscrabble landscape punctuated by the occasional family farm, school, and small town. The trip takes about four hours—three and a half at sixty-five miles per hour and no pit stops.

Because upstate real estate and living expenses are comparatively cheap, the rural counties north of Albany have become a hotbed for the local food movement. Driving north, I pass the hamlet of Shushan, New York, where Karen Weinberg makes world-class sheep's milk cheeses at 3-Corner Field Farm. Then there's Sheldon Farm in Salem, which produces varietal potatoes that are snapped up by fine restaurants in New York City.

I know I've crossed the border to Vermont not just because of the green road sign welcoming me to the state, but because the landscape suddenly changes. New York's low hills give way to dramatic, narrow valleys carved into green mountains. The landscape keeps its character almost all the way to the farm, when the high, closed-in hills unexpectedly open onto a sweeping plain. Almost as soon as it does, I spot the farm. There's our massive, white-washed 1920s barn with its shining silver cupola on my left, our red brick 1814 farmhouse and pond just beyond, and in between, a succession of matching red brick outbuildings—the corncrib, the pig house, and a second barn sitting slightly apart, overlook-ing the scene, and known as the "heifer barn" because that's where the previous owners housed their calves. And—oh yes!—there are goats, lots of goats, grazing peacefully on both sides of Vermont Route 153.

ENTERING THE FARMHOUSE, I'M GREETED BY MAYNARD, our loveable Rottweiler-Shepherd mix rescue, who catapults into me with joy when I walk through the front door. My arrival pro-vokes less enthusiasm in Pud, the most unaffectionate nonferal house cat on the planet. Pud spends the vast majority of her time dozing on the kitchen windowsill overlooking the pond. She comes to life only when she spots an opportunity to steal food from someone's plate or harass Maynard and make his life miserable.

I'm also greeted by humans. Unlike weekenders' country homes, which lay dormant throughout the workweek, except per-haps for a discreet housecleaner, my farmhouse never goes into sleep mode. Being part of a working farm, it's constantly occupied. Until very recently, our business partner, Chris Gray, lived in the house on the days I was in the city, staying in one of the guest rooms. He'd then return to Manhattan on Friday morning with our dilapidated 1996 Toyota Previa filled with cheese for New York City's weekend greenmarkets. So Chris would often be there when I walked in, sitting around the kitchen table with farmhands Margot Brooks and Alex Eaton, a delightful young couple who live in the smithy—back in the 1800s Consider Bardwell's blacksmith shop—across from the main house and hope to have their own farm someday. Margot, twenty-five, is tall with light brown hair and angelic features—which I consider entirely appropriate, since I often feel she dropped down from heaven. She's one of our cheese makers but, having grown up on a farm herself, can do just about any animal-related chore on the farm. Her boyfriend, Alex, also twenty-five, runs the barn and helps milk the goats, and is like a ray of sunshine even on the bleakest day. He's got a full head of curls, sparkly eyes, is perennially in a good mood, and treats the goats like beloved old girlfriends. And now we have Julia Bollinger, a recent graduate of Colorado College with a degree in printmaking and a mass of pre-Raphaelite curls, who lives in the house and is learning to milk goats under Alex's tutelage.

But as much as I appreciate them, and Chris too, I'll often try to drive in unobtrusively, leave my things in the car, and quietly make my rounds on the farm before anyone knows I'm there—and before they can hit me with all the questions and issues that have accumulated since I left on Monday night. I'll breathe in the fresh air, and if there's still light in the evening sky, I'll circle the house to see what perennials have bloomed during my three-day absence. Then I'll head over to the barn, where the baby goats may still be in "kindergarten"—the small, fenced-in pasture in front of the barn. I'll slip through the gate, drop to the ground, and let the babies maul me. They lick me, climb me like a hill, and chew on my hair—my expensive, city hairdo—mistaking it for grass.

If I need to be reminded of why I invest so much time and money in this crazy venture, then this—the baby goats' affection, the sun setting behind the barn, the moon rising to the east, the accompanying chorus of crickets—is all it takes.

as far as the eye can see

PEOPLE OFTEN ASK HOW A CITY GIRL LIKE ME BECAME A
goat farmer. Was there some incident that sent me down this
path, some accomplishment, such as winning a first-place 4-H
ribbon when I was ten, that could make it seem like fate?

The truth is that running a goat farm had never been on my
list of goals, but I can trace something of a path. When I was a
child growing up in the suburbs of Philadelphia, my family
bought a sweet little farm called Daisy Point when I was a
teenager. Daisy Point Farm featured an 1804 Pennsylvania stone
house and barn that had been built by a Michener, the family
who eventually adopted the little boy who became the famous
writer James Michener. We did not raise farm animals, but my

younger brother, Dan, milked cows at five o'clock every morning at a neighbor's dairy farm from the time he was twelve until he finished high school. My mother kept an extensive vegetable garden. I was acquainted with the glory of being able to go into the garden and pick a ripe tomato. She was an early proponent of going organic and an early subscriber to *Prevention* magazine. Our dinner conversations were always about clean, pesticide- and herbicide-free food. Our dinner choices focused on what vegetables were ready to be harvested. We froze much of our harvest, so that we could taste the sweet freshness of that August corn, tomatoes, and other produce in January and February.

Quite often, my father and I would spend Sunday afternoons on projects such as reroofing the springhouse, repairing a bridge over a stream in the woods, or even building stone walls in the gardens and reestablishing our orchard. I had a special little grove in our woods where I built my version of a Japanese garden. This is where I sought comfort on the day that Martin Luther King was shot. I spent the next twenty-five years romanticizing the spectacular country life of my youth and yearning to re-create it.

Even more important, I have long seen my mother's life as a cautionary tale. Despite her significant efforts at home, it had seemed that a day didn't go by that she didn't regret forsaking her talent and ambition for the yoke of a conventional 1950s homemaker. I remember often thinking—if you're so unhappy, why don't you stop complaining and just go out and pursue a career?

Eventually, when my sister, Cynthia, and I were out of the

house (I to Manhattan at age twenty-one to begin my career in publishing) and my brother, Dan, was in college, she tried. She went back to college to study horticulture. But just as she was starting to spread her wings, she discovered she had ovarian cancer. My mother was much too young when she died in her mid-fifties.

I would have been devastated at any age, but I lost her when I was twenty-eight, going through a stressful divorce, and needed her as a mentor. What saddened me most was that it happened as she was finally coming into her own. (In some small way, I am doing this farm with my mother, using my consciousness of her untapped power and curiosity to keep me going.)

That experience taught me an age-old, fundamental lesson, which has always stayed with me: If you want to accomplish something in life, don't wait. I also vowed that I would never let anyone tell me what I could and couldn't undertake.

IT WAS MY FATHER'S DEATH IN 2001 THAT PUSHED ME TO take the bigger leap of faith. When Rust, my second husband, and I bought the Vermont property that year, my main goal at that critical point was to literally and figuratively shift the scenery, to change my life somehow. For the previous twenty years, Rust and I enjoyed Manhattan life on weekdays and spent weekends and summers on Shelter Island, an eastern Long Island escape, but it seemed increasingly unfulfilling.

Shelter Island is a beautiful place, poised between the North and South Forks of Long Island, New York. It actually feels more like New England with its inlets and small, closely settled villages. But the flip side of that coziness is that everybody knows each other's business. Lovely parties, nearly nightly in August, along with sailing, drinking, dancing, and frivolous gossip increasingly seemed to consume more of my time and energy than did reading books in my hammock or taking walks at sunset along Silver Beach in the company of osprey—the reasons I was attracted to the island in the first place.

Sometimes, it takes something dramatic in your life to put things in perspective, to underline your unhappiness, to make you confront the superficiality of your life (or at least aspects of it), and that happened to me after my father's death, who suffered a hellish ten years fighting Alzheimer's. To make matters worse, I was approaching my fifties, the age my mother was when she died, and I became increasingly aware of my own mortality. Rust also hadn't been especially sympathetic to the fact that I'd had to help take care of my dad for the previous decade. On the other hand, Rust didn't get the attention he deserved during those awful years, and we were drifting apart.

I was in a personal crisis, so I attacked it the only way I know how: one hundred fifty percent. As Rust will tell you, I don't do anything halfway. When I decided to give up smoking, I went cold turkey. When I once bought an overpriced loaf of bread in Greenwich Village and then lost it while doing other errands on the way home, I was so mad at myself that I baked my own bread every day for the next year and a half. And when I decided to move on from Shelter Island, I sold the house, said my good-byes, and left. Just like that.

We—with Rust kicking and screaming but miraculously still with me—bought this huge farm and fled Shelter Island to find quiet and a new path. (At the time, I didn't understand the absurd irony of that idea. The last place on earth to get privacy is a working farm.)

On Thanksgiving weekend of 2000, we had gone to Vermont to visit some Shelter Island neighbors, Judy and Jay Inglis, who'd bought a house in the town of Dorset. For a lark, we decided to go real estate shopping. My husband's ambition was to buy a place on a river; mine was simply to start fresh. For tax reasons, we knew we needed to invest the money we'd made selling our Victorian white elephant on Shelter Island, as well as an apartment on West End Avenue in Manhattan, or else we'd have to share the profit with the IRS.

But that wasn't our only incentive. Unconsciously, both Rust and I knew that, in order to improve our marriage, we needed a new shared project. My daughter, Samantha, from my first marriage, had once shrewdly observed that for Rust and me, extended projects are like the children we never had. We were always tackling something, in the process utilizing Rust's skills as an architect and inventor and also satisfying my free-floating lapsed-Catholic guilt that compels me always to be accomplishing something. First it was our house on Shelter Island, a massive renovation project that included restoring the original porches

14

that ran along the house's first and second floors. Now it's this farm, whose demands more than exceed our collective abilities and energy.

So during that Thanksgiving weekend, we started calling realtors and surfing the Internet. When we contacted one realtor about a promising piece of property—one thousand square feet of riverfront on the Mettowee River—we were told it was no longer available. When the agent suggested we consider Bardwell farm, Rust suspected it was a case of bait-and-switch. It had no riverfront real estate, but we thought we'd check it out anyway on our way back to Manhattan.

It wasn't an auspicious beginning. We missed the turn to the farm and were anxious because we were already running late for the last ferry back to Shelter Island, a good four hours south.

When we finally found the property, we were relieved to find the owner out front sweeping. Together we surveyed the red brick farmhouse and the land behind it, which stretched almost as far as the eye could see. Rust asked her how far back the property went. "See that line of trees?" she said, pointing toward a distant ridge. "All the way there. Now, see that hill behind the trees? And the hill behind that hill?" She kept pushing the boundary back, sparking our imagination. (It also turns out to have a half-mile stretch of the Indian River running through its 305 acres, even though the house isn't on it.)

It was quite a contrast to our living situation in Shelter Island Heights. Lovely as it was, that house was almost as large as the one-eighth acre it sat on—just like all the surrounding homes.

There wasn't much breathing room. You could hear people's televisions, their toilets flushing, their occasional bickering. This farm property was the antithesis; it could be our own kingdom. I knew immediately that I wanted it. So did Rust, even though it wasn't his riverfront dream house. He'd come from a very modest British family, so it fueled his country squire fantasies. We offered the asking price the next day and closed the deal for Consider Bardwell Farm in February 2001.

My immediate ambition was to fix up the place—a monstrous undertaking in itself, since the farm had a dozen outbuildings, including two massive barns in sad states of disrepair. I also dreamed of planting a vegetable garden, having a horse, going skiing on Fridays when the Vermont slopes were empty, and hosting (select) weekend guests. I quickly dropped the horse idea after attending a care and maintenance workshop, and also realizing how much the vet would cost for every minor case of colic. As for skiing, I've had time to hit the slopes only once in the eight years since buying the farm.

Despite my urge to escape the Shelter Island social whirl, Rust and I did want to share our new adventure with people close to us. At first I was concerned that they might be reluctant to drive four-plus hours north of Manhattan—even though the three-hour trip to the Hamptons or North Fork easily becomes that long on summer Fridays, when traffic is paralyzed on the Long Island Expressway. I needn't have worried: Our farm quickly became a popular destination. People were happy to share in our "escape."

If the farm's early days are remembered for anything, it's conspicuous partying: There were cocktails and dinners and tremendous amounts of wine. After one particularly fun-loving weekend when I was away, Rust entertained a bunch of British pals, and the clean-up crew counted sixty empty bottles. (Rust became more health conscious after a scare in 2001. When he'd gone to the hospital to have a basal cell carcinoma removed, the nurses discovered that his blood pressure was so high they immediately sent him to the cardiology unit. Fortunately, medication and moderation have returned his blood pressure and cholesterol count to near-normal levels.)

Samantha's thirtieth birthday on July 2, 2001, also marked an early milestone in the annals of Consider Bardwell Farm entertaining. Previously, she had always had her party in Shelter Island, but this time the event was to be held in Vermont. More than a dozen of her friends came up from the city to help celebrate. That's when the house was truly put to the test. Unfortunately, we discovered that the septic system couldn't accommodate that much flushing. This became apparent early Saturday morning, when I woke up to the characteristic and not especially charming aroma of sewage. Luckily, the guests were still fast asleep in the house, smithy, and tents pitched across our lawns and pastures. I had no idea where the septic system was buried, though my suspicions were aroused by the sinkhole collapsed in the driveway. Leaping into action, I got out the phone book and found a listing for portable toilets. By the time Samantha and her friends awoke, a couple of Port-O-Sans were speeding to the farm.

That weekend also stands out because it was the only time a taxicab ever visited Consider Bardwell Farm—perhaps even this part of Vermont. It arrived to take away the weekend date of Valerie, one of Sam's friends from yoga class. The couple had met online, and Valerie, being something of a hippie chick, invited him along, rather than do the rational thing and first have a drink together to see whether they were as compatible in person as in cyberspace.

They were not. She was a nature girl, while he suffered something of a Woody Allen–phobia to insects and the outdoors (undoubtedly exacerbated by the fact that they were sleeping in a tent). By Saturday afternoon, this fellow—an investment banker type—had realized that Vermont's rolling hills, and possibly online dating, weren't for him. He spent several frantic hours calling taxi companies in Albany, sixty-five miles away, demanding that service be extended to our corner of Vermont. I stood by chuckling and fascinated as he negotiated the price. That was the last any of us saw of him.

THE IDEA FOR THE CHEESE FARM HAD TAKEN ROOT SHORTLY before our real estate closing in February 2001, when our realtor stopped by and presented us with a history of the property. As it turns out, Consider Bardwell, our farm's namesake, was quite an entrepreneurial fellow. In the early 1800s, he manufactured edge tools such as axes, owned a nearby slate quarry, lived in our sturdy red brick house, and dug a pond whose runoff supplied enough power to operate his machinery. Five decades later, in March 1864, Bardwell established Vermont's very first cheese co-op, a predecessor of Cabot Creamery, in a barnlike structure that burned down in 2000.

The Nelsonville Cheese Factory, as it was called after the Nelson family bought the property in the late 1860s, was a boon to local farmers, because it gave them an outlet for their surplus milk. Their wives were perhaps even happier: Sending the milk away relieved them of the burden of turning it into butter and cheese. Soon after we bought the farm, I met one of these women, who was in her late nineties. She remembered delivering milk to our farm as a child with her grandfather in their horse-drawn wagon.

A light went on in my head when I read about the cheese factory, which endured until the 1930s, when the Great Depression killed it. What if we resurrected the dairy and manufactured cheese ourselves?

Even though I really enjoyed the farm as a retreat, it was this thought that stuck with me and at last galvanized me, like a magnet drawing together metal shards; all of the disparate forces in my life seemed to align. It didn't take much to talk myself into believing that cheese was part of my karma. When I was a child, my mother often called me "Mouse" because I liked cheese so much. But I was certainly no connoisseur; Velveeta would do. I loved the way it melted on my tongue. And when I moved to New York City in the early '70s and eventually to Manhattan's Upper West Side, I toyed with the idea of opening my own cheese shop. I used to haunt the cheese aisle of Zabar's, the famed specialty-food store, and linger over its hundreds of beautifully wrapped cheeses, studying the musky, moldy, pungent, and aromatic bundles.

Rust was inspired, too. We knew we needed to do a lot of work. We set out to educate ourselves about farming in general and cheese making in particular. When we went to Tuscany for two weeks at the end of the summer of 2001, it was for a much-needed vacation, not to pick up cheese-making tips from the Italians. But we couldn't help ourselves. Our farm, waiting back in Vermont, felt like the key to a new life, a new adventure. Suddenly we were more interested in how Tuscan farmers baled their hay and what sort of animals they were raising than in the frescoes and churches of Florence and Siena.

We got grief from friends who joined us. When they came from New York or London to visit us at Mandorlo, the large villa in Pienza we rented from legendary New York editor Larry Ashmead, they teased us about our newfound fascination with things like crop rotation. They'd come to Italy to hang out at Montepulciano's wine bars and admire the setting sun, not to quiz the locals on their field-tilling techniques.

Rust and I spent the next two years going to farming symposia and conferences. We took cheese-making workshops, including a weeklong course on British cheese making taught by Kathy Biss, a famous Scottish cheese maker. Rust did very well, better than I did—or ever will.

Despite my deep-seated love for cheese, I admit that cheese making isn't my strength. I can certainly make simple, tasty fresh cheese at home and have become astute about the process of cheese making, but I don't have the patience to spend weeks and months experimenting with cultures and temperatures, and adjusting the recipe for the changing fat and protein content of milk from season to season. Nor do I care to stand over a hot cheese vat, stirring several hours a day, so I knew enough to hire cheese makers.

Many people fantasize about making excellent cheeses in small batches, keeping only a few goats and doing much of the labor themselves or with one or two helpers. My ambition—and Rust's, I might add—quickly became something more expensive: to build a world-class cheese company.

In that regard, we urban professionals who come to farming at midlife might bring something that generational farmers might not: a business vision, marketing skills, and perhaps a somewhat more sophisticated palate. Conversely, we lack the vast knowledge base, wisdom, and experience that get passed down from one generation of family farmers to the next.

Agenting books is a snap compared to the range of skills required to successfully operate the kind of farm we have. You have to be part veterinarian, biologist, small business owner, animal husbandry expert, farm tour guide, and more.

Of course, my food industry connections were helpful in a limited way. By the time we bought the farm, I was quite active in the New York City food community, agenting books for such famous chefs as Jean-Georges Vongerichten, owner of more than a dozen restaurants in Manhattan and around the world, and Marcus Samuelsson of Aquavit and other restaurants. Another of my authors was Max McCalman, one of the world's leading cheese experts and the maître fromager at critically acclaimed Manhattan restaurant Picholine. He definitely nurtured my cheese dreams. But I've rarely tried to exploit my food-industry connections. Just the opposite, in fact. I'm afraid that if my clients discover I've been playing hooky for half the week up on the farm, they'll find a new agent. I still don't think Jean Georges Vongerichten knows that some of the cheese he sells at Jean Georges, his three-star restaurant, comes from his agent's farm.

Mark Bittman, another client of mine and the author of such best-selling cookbooks as *How to Cook Everything* as well as *The New York Times* "Minimalist" columnist, told me that he was having lunch at Jean Georges recently when they brought out the cheese plate. One of the cheeses was so delicious that Mark asked Jean-Georges what it was. "It's from *Vrai-mont,*" is all the French chef could tell him. So Jean-Georges sent for his brother Philippe, the restaurant's manager. Philippe came out and explained that the cheese was West Pawlet Quarry (we've since renamed it Chester), our natural bloomed rind, soft raw cow's milk cheese.

"Did you know this is Angela's cheese?" Mark asked Jean-Georges.

Mark doesn't think the information registered with Jean-Georges. He's a whirlwind, always on to the next thing, which helps explain his success. But from my point of view, it's just as well he forgets—at least, as long as he keeps buying my cheese. I wouldn't want him worrying that I'm milking goats when I should be coming up with a deal for his next big book.

farm team

THE HARDEST THING I'VE HAD TO OVERCOME ON THE FARM is the suspicion from my own employees that I'm a dilettante. It doesn't seem to matter how many eighteen-hour days I've logged over the last eight years, or how much money I've spent on equipment, infrastructure, and staff. Some of those employees still don't take me entirely seriously. They think this is some sort of folly. Considering themselves authentic country folk who hunt and fish and know their way around animals, they feel their judgments and insights are superior to my own.

"You have your farm for fun," one of our teenage farmhands told me dismissively a few days after a major argument about the way we were separating newborn kids from their mothers immediately after birth. "And you have your real job in the city."

Rarely was that dismissive attitude more evident than during the 2008 kidding season—to my mind the official start of the cheese-making year—when an explosive dispute erupted after one of our favorite goats, Lailani, gave birth. This was right at the beginning of kidding season, a busy time that lasts about six weeks. Goats become pregnant in November and have a five-month gestation period. The first of the "girls," as we affectionately call them, goes into labor beginning in late March, and the last gives birth by early May.

Lailani was one of our more senior and weaker does, and she had found a spot in the back pasture to go through labor. Her back legs didn't work that well, so she spent a lot of time lying down. It made sense that she'd remove herself from the herd to give birth. Goats prefer to be alone when they deliver their babies, away from the rest of the herd, and in her compromised condition, Lailani had better reason than most to seek isolation. Survival of the fittest applies as much to the barnyard as it does to the wild. Strong goats dominate the weak and sometimes butt heads to establish their dominance. Earlier, we had to move her into the kids' pen because the other goats were beating her so badly that we were afraid she would miscarry. When Lailani nears her turn in the milk line, we'll often find her hiding from the other milkers, who might otherwise pick on her. She'll linger in a vestibule outside the holding pen that leads to the milking parlor, waiting until the last shift and entering with the youngest and lowest-ranking goats. Sometimes we'll even have to fetch her from the loafing yard behind the barn and lead her inside.

The kidding dispute started after Debbie Tracy reported there was a goat in the back pasture in heavy labor. Debbie, who worked in our cheese room, was a slim, fiftyish "mean country redneck," by her own description, with her name tattooed on her hand. She was a quick study who could have run the farm by herself after working for us for only a few months, and she helped us deliver babies because she'd once had her own goat dairy. Given her knowledge about animal husbandry and goats in particular, I knew I could rely on her to help with any difficult births or kidding crises.

Debbie found me in the barn busy helping midwife three goats in the throes of labor. I was assisting Laura Fletcher, another key staffer during the kidding season. Laura is an optometrist and licensed nurse by profession, but she loves goats, especially baby goats, and had come up from Texas for the second year in a row to help with the kidding. She'd found us in August 2006 after Googling "goat internships." Laura, a round, five-feet one-inch figure—whose agenda might not have included losing significant amounts of weight while she was with us, but nonetheless did—drove two thousand two hundred miles in seven days, visiting farms from Maryland to Maine, before deciding that ours was the most pleasant.

Laura and I rushed down to the pasture and saw that it was Lailani in labor. She had already given birth to two underweight babies: a boy and a girl with strange, floppy ears. (The ears of an Oberhasli, the Swiss Alpine breed we raise, are supposed to stand up straight.) A third baby was on the way.

At the stern urging of our vet, Dr. Amanda Alderink, Laura and I had decided to do things a little differently this year: We would remove the babies from their moms at the moment of birth. In dairy-goat parlance, it's called "pulling." Dr. Alderink stressed that if we separated them quickly, before they could form a bond, the newborns would suffer far fewer of the problems that crop up when you leave them on their moms. Debbie disapproved; she used to keep her babies on the moms for two or three days before she pulled them. But for the most part, she kept her own counsel.

Because we were suddenly faced with seven simultaneous births, we had been joined by Sandy Martin, a neighbor who raises a few sheep and has a way with animals. During this period, she'd been hired to do chores in the barn every afternoon. Sandy, rakishly thin with a boy's buzz cut, had already run to Lailani's side and was lying on the ground beside her, letting the goat lick her babies clean. But Sandy wasn't part of our kidding team, so she hadn't been consulted or informed about our decision to promptly remove the babies from their mothers.

When I arrived, I asked Leslie Goff, who at age eighteen had worked on the farm side for four years and had recently transitioned to the cheese room, to take Lailani's first two babies back to the barn, wrap them up, and put them into a little cradle to wait until we could attend to them. That's when Sandy decided to challenge my credentials as an authentic farmer. She wasn't happy that we were taking the babies away from their mothers so soon after birth. "This is unconscionable," she said. "I can't work here. I can't do this." And just like that, she got up from Lailani's side to leave. Sandy was due to move on to another job several days later anyway, so our tempest merely hastened her departure. I swallowed my impulse to strangle her—several obscenities hung on the tip of my tongue. But my training in publishing's corporate trenches had taught me to curb my temper. I offered her a clipped thank you and wished her well.

Pulling the babies wasn't some whimsical decision on my part. The year before, my maternal instincts had won out, and I'd let the mothers remain with their babies until they were weaned, about eight weeks. But as I learned, that goes against the advice of most expert dairy farmers and vets, who tell you to separate mother and newborn before they develop a bond—and for good reason.

If you are raising goats for dairy production and ultimately to make cheese, letting nature take its course comes at substantial cost to the cheese-making operation. For those two months, every drop of milk the mother produces goes to her babies instead of the cheese. And at the end of that time, the bond between mother goat and kid has grown so strong that separating them can be even more traumatic than when it's done at birth. The babies will be unfriendly with their human handlers.

Even before the disagreement about pulling Lailani's kids, authority had been a recurring issue. When we started making cheese in 2003, many of our workers knew more than my husband and I did—and felt a continual obligation to tell us so.

Admittedly, the learning curve is steep for anyone starting a farm. At the beginning, I certainly did want people around me who were more knowledgeable, but after six years of kidding and learning, I'd seen everything and could increasingly trust my own instincts. So I made peace with the decision to separate the babies from the mothers as quickly as possible and let my opinionated employees know that I'd deal with any consequences.

THIS NEW SEASON, WE HOPED FINALLY TO BREAK EVEN with the cheese business, perhaps even turn a profit. Crucial to that was doubling our cheese production. To achieve that goal, we knew we'd need every ounce of milk we could get from our own herd, plus we'd made a deal to purchase the entire production of Polymeadows Farm & Creamery, a nearby two hundred and forty–goat dairy beginning May 1. Their milk would be used to make our Manchester tomme, a nutty, earthy cheese named for the town that's the gateway to the Green Mountains in Vermont. We were also buying cow's milk from Jersey Girls, another farm, to make cow's milk cheese, and Rust was putting the finishing touches on a second cheese-ripening room.

After much turnover, we also finally assembled a first-rate team. That is perhaps the accomplishment of which I'm most proud. It isn't easy to staff a farm. What sounds like it ought to be an oasis of Zen-like calm, a refuge from the pace and problems of modern life, has its own stresses. Everybody has to pull her or his own weight. There's no such thing as "later" when it comes to milking animals or making cheese. If one person has a tendency to let things slide, somebody else had better be there to pick up the slack. Some parts of the operation—the cheese-making room and the cheese-aging cave, in particular—require employees to work in close proximity for hours at a time.

Peter Dixon, our world-class cheese maker, leads the team. A native Vermonter, Peter teaches workshops on cheese making and starting your own cheese business, and has consulted from China to Kosovo.

On the business side is Chris Gray, who has primary responsibility for selling to restaurants and wholesalers, and for managing the dozen farmers' markets we attend from Vermont to New York City. Chris is a former music-industry executive; the talent he once used to promote recording artists he's now applying to marketing our Manchester, Pawlet, and Dorset cheeses. "I'm the moneymaker," he joked at a party celebrating Vermont cheeses at Martha Stewart's Lower West Side offices. "I turn yellow into green." He and his wife, Laura Brown, who also works in the recording industry, recently bought a house in West Pawlet and eventually hope to move there permanently from Brooklyn.

Rust is confident we're going to succeed, that it's all in the cards, for this simple reason: Every time we've lost an important staff member and thought the farm's future was in peril, someone even better came along.

That was the case when Debbie Tracy quit in June 2008, after working for us for less than a year. She lived near Middlebury and commuted to the farm every day in her pickup truck, a round-trip journey of approximately fifty-five miles. She wanted an additional $200 a week to offset the cost of gas, which had soared past $4 a gallon. Since we were always strapped for cash, I instead offered her the use of my cute little 1993 cherry-red Miata, at least during the summer months when the weather was good. But she turned the offer down, saying she felt safer in her truck, and left us shortly afterward.

Then along came Margot Brooks. She had just graduated from St. Lawrence University and wanted to intern on a goat cheese farm. She came from an old farming family—five generations had run a cow dairy near Cooperstown, New York—and Margot's ambition was to spend a few years learning the goat cheese business, then join her family's operation and add a cow's milk and goat's milk cheese-making creamery. I offered her a modest weekly salary, plus the use of the smithy, the small house across the front yard, which came with a wood-burning stove. Thrown into the deal was all the cheese she might want. She accepted and quickly became an accomplished cheese maker, despite the enormous pressure everyone was under as we ramped up production. She wasn't the only novice. Leslie Goff, our third cheese maker, was a local college student who was learning on the job and becoming possibly the youngest professional cheese maker in Vermont. Our herd manager was also in training: That was Margot's boyfriend, Alex Eaton, who moved into the smithy in September.

Then there were the local teenagers who worked on the farm

side. There was Leslie's best friend, Minny Buley. At age nineteen, Minny might have the sharpest tongue in this part of Vermont, but she was an incredibly hard worker. She frequently offered to go to her Jeep and get her shotgun if we ever needed to put a goat down (but politely vanished the time she was actually offered the opportunity to put an ailing goat out of its misery). She joined us at the start of kidding season and shared the barn work with Alex.

Amber Goff was sixteen and Leslie's first cousin. I knew I could always count on her in a crunch, even though she also worked a second job at AJ's Fine Food and Spirits in Granville, New York, when she wasn't in school or competing on the boys' wrestling team—and Amber had the biceps, or "pipes" as Minny called them, to prove it. When she started working for us, I asked her whether she thought she could lift a forty-four-pound bale of hay. "I can press a hundred," she stated confidently. She was thirteen at the time.

OUR TEAM WAS EAGER, HARDWORKING, AND CAPABLE, BUT not always thrilled about following orders. During kidding season in 2008, our budding cheese maker Leslie would provide me with an opportunity—though one I didn't relish—to test my muscular new management style.

The day after the argument over Lailani's delivery, Leslie emerged from the barn in tears saying she couldn't work with Laura. It seems the Texan goat-midwife had provoked an argument over something silly: She criticized the way Leslie screwed the caps onto the feeding bottles, contending that her method risked collapsing the nipples, which would allow air to enter the kids' lungs. Maybe Laura was right, maybe not, but she didn't have much appreciation for the younger generation, so I suspect she corrected the eighteen-year-old in a high-handed way that left little doubt that she considered teenagers in general, and Leslie in particular, moody pains in the ass. Leslie had bottle-fed baby goats hundreds of times, but Laura, now charged with the responsibility, decided to throw her weight around.

It bugged Laura to hear "this is the way my grandfather always did it." Some of the kids who work here have grown up on family farms, and they sometimes do things without ever questioning conventional wisdom. While this area of Vermont and nearby New York State attracts a fair number of cosmopolitan artists and wealthy second-homeowners, the locals remain proudly provincial. They refer to themselves as rednecks. They know how to ride horses and snowmobiles, fix milking-machine pumps and motors, and are willing to scrub a milk bulk tank until it's spanking clean—and they follow the rituals they've long known.

Rust, amusingly cynical, has a simple solution when I complain about friction between employees: "Fire the lot of them." New York City's ambitious young foodies would kill for the kind of real-world experience our people are getting (and Laura might have preferred working with them.) There's only one problem: Those twentysomething liberal arts majors don't live in rural Vermont. They live in hip, edgy communities like Williamsburg in Brooklyn and Hoboken, New Jersey. And manure on your boots 24/7 gets tiresome quickly. The local teenagers and college kids whom we hire live here, have their own cars, and show up at the crack of dawn to milk the goats or crank up the cheese-making equipment. Sometimes these kids even profess gratitude for having a job.

When Laura challenged Leslie's way of screwing the caps onto feeding bottles, the young cheese maker, who was trying to help out, launched into a litany of complaints—not just about her older colleague, but also she too brought up the way we were pulling the newborns off their mothers. "It's like Debbie said yesterday," Leslie announced earnestly, sounding very much like a teenager. "It's like somebody took the baby! It's like it's not safe to have another baby."

I made it clear that I didn't like the sniping. I wasn't hosting a house party or running an animal shelter. People had been hired to do a job. I asked Laura to apologize and she did. Leslie quieted down. After that, she and Laura simply gave each other a wide berth, with Leslie taking comfort in the knowledge that Laura would be returning to Texas in another month, once the kidding season wound down.

The one person on whom my budding farm-management skills don't work is my husband. Rust was up front about having no interest in or intention of caring for animals. At the outset of this endeavor, he tried mightily to get me to think about how much work a dairy farm entailed. (He failed on that score.) But even though he's not a farmer, there's no way we could have gotten this far without his skills and imagination.

Rust is an integral part of the team, but he marches to the beat of his own drum. He'll spend a good couple of hours every morning checking out his favorite political websites and British football scores. But then he'll throw himself into some elaborate farm repair or construction. Though trained as an architect, he's a better plumber and electrician than most people who earn a living at it. At Consider Bardwell Farm, but he has not only renovated the house, barns, and outbuildings, but he's also built the two cheese-ripening rooms. What's more, he's done so in such imaginative, energy-saving ways that we've been praised by Efficiency Vermont, a cutting-edge nonprofit that provides energy solutions to homes and businesses. The organization has given us several grants and even asked Rust to consider doing more work with them. We've also qualified for numerous government grants because of him. His latest project is to attach solar collectors to the barn's towering silo. Electricity from the panels would not only heat the huge water tanks inside the silo, but also chill water and pump it through pipes to cool the cheese rooms.

And there are other, less tangible areas where Rust's support has been vital. In the bedroom at 4 A.M., but not necessarily in the way that immediately comes to mind. That's when I start whimpering. And I don't mean that figuratively. I mean actual sounds. I admit it's a strange noise to imagine coming from a normally calm, confident woman, over and over again. But it's involuntary, the result of the near relentless pressure I put myself under. I'll wake up plagued by a stream of terrible thoughts, such as "We're going to run out of money; the little goat with a limp isn't getting any better and may die; the yearlings across the street need their bedding changed; the Vermont farmers' markets have ended for the season so there will be $2,000 less every week to pay bills; might the coyotes I hear howling in the distance be preparing to attack the milkers in the pasture; is Alex remembering to sprinkle kelp on the milkers' grain ration; oh my god, we're going to have so many babies next April, how am I going to get rid of all but twenty of them?"

It could be only one of those thoughts, all of them, or others that set me off. I'll be curled in a fetal position on my left side: my favorite position for sleeping, when the whimpering starts. It wakes Rust up and he chivalrously takes on my anxiety, gets out of bed, and goes to the kitchen for a soothing cup of tea, all the while muttering about whatever it was that set me off. My worries now safely transferred to him, I'm able to go back to sleep until the alarm goes off at 6 A.M.

One of Rust's frequent middle-of-the-night suggestions is to find a way to cut back our payroll, especially since, no matter how many people we have working for us, I'm often the employee who ends up performing the farm's most menial chores. "Why are we paying all these people?" my husband barked one afternoon in not entirely mock outrage to some weekend guests, after he returned from the barn, where he had counted a small army of laborers. "Angela's literally shoveling the shit."

35

IN A SENSE, EVEN WORKING IN THE BARN, ANKLE DEEP IN dung, is a labor of love—because I love our goats, the most significant members of the team. We purchased our original six Oberhasli, or Swiss Alpine goats, in August 2003. They were from a show goat farm in Dunbarton, New Hampshire, that was known for producing goat beauty queen champions. And Oberhaslis are adorable. They're typically brown, though the official description is "bay" or "chamoisee," and have cute black knee socks, a black stripe running down their back, and erect ears. Choosing the Oberhasli breed was the idea of our first employee, Marie Louise Ryan, as she'd raised them in France where she was a goatherd and cheese maker. That first day with the goats was a memorable one. I'd never been in the same car with one goat, let alone six. In fact, I'd never even met a goat until we went to look at these girls. Marie Louise was doing the driving, while I fenced off the front seat with my arm to prevent them from joining us there. I didn't even know whether they'd bite me or not. (They do nibble on your nose and hair, but not aggressively. I know now that's just to get to know you. Like toddlers, they'll put their mouths on anything.)

If I'd known better, I would have borrowed a livestock trailer. Instead, Marie Louise and I rented a minivan from National Car Rental in Rutland, Vermont, about forty miles away. We picked up the girls, who ranged in age from four months to two years—Petunia, Victoria, Zena, Magnolia, Iris, and Lily—and drove home.

Little did I know we were committing a crime: transporting live-stock across state lines without a veterinarian's release.

We had also committed another transgression—against the car rental company. When picking up the van, I lied and said we needed to transport some precious family heirlooms. Then I removed the back seats, lined the bottom of the vehicle with a tarp, and sprinkled hay on top. The idea was to make the six goats feel at home and also to absorb any bodily fluids they might produce en route.

And produce they did. When goats get nervous, they tend to pee. These gals, struggling to stay upright during our stop-and-go drive through scenic Vermont at the height of tourist season, peed copiously and not necessarily on the tarp.

That evening, I scrubbed the minivan furiously with Mr. Clean and let it air out overnight. When I returned it the next day, I strategically parked it in a remote corner of the lot, as far away from the rental-agency office as possible, praying they wouldn't notice the barnyard bouquet. And they didn't. At least they never contacted me. I took that as a good omen.

WE CAN'T FORGET BOB HAHN, OUR FIFTY-ONE-YEAR-OLD maintenance man, who is there for us in so many ways. One of his signature accomplishments was during this critical year, 2008. In anticipation of the birth of at least eighty kids, he had constructed what we affectionately came to call the Stairway to

Heaven: a miniature flight of stairs that the babies could use to access the outdoors from the baby pen inside the barn.

By the end of that first week of kidding in March, we were ready to try it out. It was a Sunday, and the gloomy gray clouds that had covered the Mettowee Valley for days had broken. A dazzling spring sun had emerged; winter's lingering chill seemed finally to have fled. So we carried the babies up the staircase and introduced them to the world.

For a while, they wouldn't budge from the small bridge that spanned the short distance from the window threshold to the ground. They were intimidated by the newness of their surroundings, not the height. Goats love to climb and jump and climb again, over and over. But their curiosity got the better of them, along with our pleas and a gentle push. Eventually, they ventured out into a small fenced-in pasture—their kindergarten—though never straying too far from Laura and me, their surrogate mothers. They quickly began following me wherever I went, and when I sat down on the grass, they overwhelmed me, climbing into my lap, licking my face, and tugging at my hair. I loved their enthusiastic affection. They might never say "mom," but playful, loving kids of any kind (perhaps of any species) are hard to resist.

Meanwhile, Rust was taking advantage of their absence to install an automatic milk dispenser called the Lac-Tek, which we were using for the first time. It's an attention-getting device that comes with six highly realistic-looking udders; there's a little pink nipple on each. Rust had leapt into action after I reminded him how much money we could save if we didn't have to hire people to bottle-feed the babies. Since he had helped me do the midnight feeding the night before—between the two of us, we bottle-fed thirty-seven babies from midnight to 3 A.M.—he had personal motivation.

Within an hour, Rust had drilled six perfect holes through a rectangular sheet of plywood, inserted one of the Lac-Tek's provocative plastic teats into each, and run tubes back to the machine, which I'd dubbed the Magic Mother. We introduced this marvel to the babies a few days later.

The Lac-Tek machine in a sense became an essential part of our farm team, but like everything else associated with Consider Bardwell Farm, it came with a precipitous learning curve, and with consequences we hadn't foreseen.

FOUR

the new kids

BABY GOATS ARE ABLE TO STAND ON THEIR OWN TO NURSE by the time they're a few minutes old. Those survival instincts also mean they're immediately quite insistent about being fed. If their mother's udder isn't available at all times, there had better be an alternative.

Ever since 2004, when we delivered the first babies on the farm, the drill has gone something like this: A few days before delivery, we shave the moms' udders to ensure cleaner milk. In exchange for making them suffer this indignity, I give each doe a handful of raisins—the equivalent of luscious Godiva chocolate to a goat. Those treats are surpassed only by the molasses-sweetened grain pellets used to lure the goats into the milking parlor twice a day. Since there are only fourteen milking stations, we can't let the entire herd of several dozen goats in at once. But those grain pellets work all too well. It takes all of our strength and agility to prevent the gals from barreling through the holding-pen gate at the same time.

Shortly after delivery, we milk the mothers for their colostrum, a thick, yellowish milk secreted after giving birth that's high in antibodies. The extracted mother's milk is put in baby bottles—the same kind used by humans, with the same type of nipple. It's warmed to 103°F, the equivalent of a doe's fresh milk, then fed to the newborns every four hours for the first three days. Eventually that gets reduced to six hours, then to three times a day, then two, until they're weaned after approximately eight weeks. After weaning, a kid's diet consists entirely of water, hay, pasture grasses, and about a cup of grain.

Laura made the hand-milking job much easier by sourcing a device that is like a human breast pump adapted for goats. Since the plastic cylinder that fits onto the goat's teat is sanitary and never touched by human hands, it has the added advantage of keeping the milk as bacteria- and contaminant-free as possible.

Among those pushy, early babies jockeying to be first fed were Lailani's triplets: a girl and two boys. The boys were small, but the girl was even tinier, no more than four pounds. A typical healthy kid can weigh double or even triple that at birth. So for the first twenty-four hours, we had our doubts about whether the doeling, christened Flopsy by Leslie because of her uncharacteristically floppy ears, would make it.

It almost seemed as if the ears weren't the result of faulty genes. (Oberhasli ears are characteristically perky and upright.) Instead, it appeared that whatever limited energy Lailani could lend her babies wasn't sufficient to make Flopsy's ears stand up. But as it turned out, Flopsy's survival instincts—which included an ability to charm—were as strong as any animal's in the barn.

Flopsy and her siblings were members of the third generation of goats raised on Consider Bardwell Farm. Lailani is the daughter of Zena, one of the six original goats bought in New Hampshire in 2003. We have a closed herd, which means that we have not introduced new does into the group since I acquired a dozen more from the same farm the following spring: five milkers and seven yearlings. All subsequent goats are their offspring, born and bred on the farm.

Unless an Oberhasli has especially distinctive markings, which is rare, it's hard to distinguish one from the other, so we give them permanent identification collars. If a baby loses her collar, there's almost no way of knowing who she is. So we also tattoo the kids— the final step in the kidding process—when they're about twelve weeks old. After naming and listing the goats and their mothers, the youngsters get an American Dairy Goat Association–approved ID number in each ear. The number of our farm, 5 AM, is tattooed in one ear. In the other goes their individual number. In 2008, every ID started with the letter Y. For example, Honey, daughter of Sugar and the first doe born this year, bears the tattoo Y1. Forever after, goats will not let you play with their ears.

I also like to give the mothers and daughters related names to help keep their lineage straight in my overburdened mind. So Petunia's offspring are named after flowers beginning with the letter *P*: Sweet Pea, Phlox, Peony, and Posey. Victoria's line features names from English royalty: Princess Elizabeth, Princess Anne, and Lady Diana.

I plead guilty to playing favorites with my goats. There's a black doe named Koh-i-Noor, Koko for short, whom I simply adore. (I'm absurdly partial to black Oberhaslis, who are the result of a recessive gene, like blue eyes in humans.) Koko has a distinctive white diamond blaze on her forehead. A friend was visiting the day she was born and duly christened her Koh-i-Noor, after the 105-carat Star of India, once the largest diamond in the world.

Koko is as close to a pet as I have in the herd. She follows me around like a shadow and behaves as though she deserves special treatment, which I sometimes grant. When I made the decision this year to pull the babies off their mothers at birth, Koko was one of the does who protested the loudest. It was as if she, like the farmhands, was testing my authority, albeit from a more personal perspective; she seemed to be letting me know that I had no business telling a goat how to raise her young. She apparently thought that, given our special relationship, if she cried long and loud enough, I'd give her babies back. In fact, she cried so much she lost her voice.

As it turned out, she had a point about goats being the greater expert with newborn kids. A few days later, I was standing by the kids' pen making lists of all the babies in order to get them permanent identification collars. I heard a small, unusual sound. It came from a little brown girl who was standing behind the Stairway to Heaven. I kept working, but then she cried again; this time I realized that she was clearly suffering. I jumped into the pen, carried her out, and realized that her belly was hard as a rock and about four times its normal size. She was extremely bloated.

Bloat is a problem goats face when they eat too much and their rumen fills with gas. Goat stomachs have four chambers, and the first, the rumen, acts as a fermentation vat, using bacteria and enzymes to break down the fiber that older goats dine on: grass, hay, and sometimes the neighbor's hydrangeas. When a goat is a baby, however, its rumen is tiny and undeveloped. That's why it depends on milk rather than roughage for its food source.

Before Laura left when the kidding season was done, she fixed me up with a "bloat kit" in anticipation of just such a problem. It consisted of a syringe and a bloat-control liquid called, appropriately enough, Bloat-Aid. I asked Corey Chapin, one of the farm's young workers, to pour the bloat cocktail down her throat using a syringe while I held her still. As he did, her ears went back, her little head flopped sideways, and she went limp. She may have died of a heart attack from the pressure of the bloated belly and the stress of resisting our application of the medication.

As traumatic as the incident was—the baby was the daughter of Nadia, one of my quietest and most productive milkers—we put her body in a plastic bag (for sanitary reasons) to be buried by Bob Hahn, and I went back to what I had been doing. These horrible tragedies happen on a farm, fortunately not very often, but you try not to dwell on them. Except then I heard another baby cry. I turned around and saw that a second kid had the same problem. This time it was a little black kid, one of Princess Anne's twins. She was a skinny little goat, but her sides were bulging and she was whimpering in pain.

I picked up the phone and called Sue Olsen, our farm manager at the time. Sue had been with us for a little over a month and previously had some experience working with a vet. I asked her to rush over. I also called the vet's office but was told they couldn't get anybody to the farm in less than forty minutes. The kid was in such distress, I didn't think she'd last that long. The only other person in the barn besides Corey was Chris Gray, who was in the cheese-packing room getting ready to do the weekly sales trek to New York City.

Chris recalled a conversation he had heard between Laura and the vet about bloat. The vet had said that an emergency measure to release some of the gas would be to stick a needle gently into the goat's side. It sounded gruesome, but the poor thing was in such pain and the procedure could provide instant relief. You make a hole in the animal's flank with an 18-gauge needle, then insert a tube or straw to release the gas.

Soon, Sue arrived. She got a needle and syringe, stuck it into the kid's rumen, and we heard the hissing of released air. If nothing else, we'd bought some time until the vet arrived. When Dr. Alderink finally came, she inserted a long tube through the mouth, past the gag reflex, and down toward the baby's stomach.

However, the stomach was so blocked by the gassy, frothy material that the vet had trouble fully inserting the tube. She was finally able to reach the stomach and attached a big syringe to the tube, then shot a cocktail of charcoal, oil, Pepto-Bismol, penicillin, and aspirin down the baby's throat. By this time, the kid had gone from looking alert and painfully sick to barely moving. Dr. Alderink said there was nothing else we could do, except hope for the best.

The baby lingered in that state through the next evening. I came to agree with Debbie Tracy, who had raised goats for many years, that the only humane thing to do was to euthanize it. Farmers keep guns handy for such cases. But the only gun we had was an air rifle that Rust used for target practice on rats in the chicken coop. Besides, even if I'd had a gun and knew how to use it, I still wouldn't have been able to pull the trigger. The whimpering baby was so small and hurt that all I could do was sob for it. I couldn't and still can't bring myself to personally euthanize a sick animal. I can't even kill a spider (although flies and mosquitoes are fair game). But I couldn't kill this poor little baby, even though she was suffering beyond anything I'd ever seen. Debbie suggested that Chris do the task with a hammer or a rock.

Chris, a city boy who lives in Brooklyn for most of the week, probably had never imagined that this would be part of his job as a business manager. But he surprised me by readily agreeing to put the animal out of its misery. So while I stood on one side of our delivery truck, hands covering my ears, Chris stood on the other side and, as swiftly and mercifully as he could, whacked a concrete block against the kid's head.

The next morning, he recounted a nightmare about someone trying to shoot him. Even though he did what had to be done, it clearly haunted him.

Though we're still not sure of the reason for the bloating—three other kids came down with it, but less severely—the reason was most likely our new Lac-Tek machine. Maybe the milk replacer was too concentrated. Or maybe the babies didn't know when to stop guzzling. We thought the Lac-Tek nurser would be more natural than bottle-feeding. And if we'd let them stay on their mothers, they'd also have been free to feed whenever they wanted. The difference is that their mother (as Koko may have been trying to tell me) gently pushes them away when she decides they've had enough. The Lac-Tek isn't so savvy. Also, it was mid-May and the pasture grass was new and rich, and the kids were now eating a lot of that, too. The vet and I agreed that it must have been a lethal combination of too much rich milk and green grass filling the belly.

In the wake of those deaths, we severely restricted the kids' access to the machine, letting them feed from it only twice a day rather than whenever they wanted, and for only two minutes at a time. The Lac-Tek was no longer really needed, in any case—at least for this year. The older babies, born in early April, were now nearly eight weeks old. It was almost time for them to stop drinking milk altogether and graduate to grain. Weaning took place swiftly after the bloat attacks.

AS CUTE AND ENDEARING AS BABY GOATS ARE, I HAVE TO force myself not to bond with the newborn boys. This time there were forty-four of them. They would all be leaving shortly because, sadly, they didn't have a future on the farm. We had three breeding bucks—Boris, Kennedy, and Tyrone—but that's all we needed. I had a meeting set up at Polymeadows Farm in Shaftsbury, Vermont, about thirty minutes away, to sell nine four-day-old boys to Betsy Sinclair, a nearby farmer who raises young bucklings for kid meat. Polymeadows, which supplied us with the milk we use to make our Manchester cheese, was also selling Barbara some of its baby males, so we decided to rendezvous there.

In previous years, I had tried to find a home for every boy. In 2004, the first season we had babies, we had only one, which I had wethered and kept. We named him Geoffrey, after Rust's brother-in-law, who had died the week before the kid was born. Wethers— or neutered bucks—have their uses, as we discovered when we bought our first breeding buck, Madison, and put him in a pen by himself. Goats are herd animals, and they don't do well being alone. For Madison, that was the equivalent of solitary confinement, and overnight he spiraled into a depression so severe that he refused to stand up. So we put Geoffrey in with him, and Madison's spirits quickly revived. Geoffrey became Madison's significant other.

The following year, we had eight or nine boys, and I found adoptive homes for most and sold the others for breeding stock. Last year, I gave some of the boys away as pets and sold the rest. But this year, we were expecting so many babies I knew I wouldn't have time to find the boys a home. Besides, I needed to give my undivided attention to the girls, the future milkers of Consider Bardwell Farm.

One cheese-making farmer I know cuts the boys' throats as soon as they're born and adds their little bodies to the compost pile. Another farmer takes most of her babies to the livestock auction each Tuesday during kidding season and sells them for about fifty cents each. Many farmers likely follow either of these methods and I've come to understand the practical reason, but I have to live with myself, and I comfort myself knowing that our little bucklings will have some purpose in life, even if it's only as meat.

Having said that, I had fresh misgivings when I delivered the first of the boys to Betsy Sinclair this year to be slaughtered.

The nine young bucks, the first of this kidding season's males, made the trip in a crowded basket in the back of my SUV, but didn't utter a single bleat of protest or alarm. Like human babies, for them the soft whir of the wheels, the gentle motion of the car, and the passing Vermont landscape must have lulled them into silent appreciation. Certainly, they seemed to have no sense of their fate.

We arrived at the farm, and I was distracted for a moment by the spectacular views looking south toward Bennington, Vermont. Betsy was chatting with Polymeadows' Melvin and Jennifer Lawrence, all of them standing beside her mud-caked pickup truck. The gamey goat smell in the back of the truck, crowded with dozens of male kids of a half-dozen breeds and colors, lingered in my nostrils for hours afterward. I don't believe that just because you work on a farm with animals means that their scent need permeate every fiber of your existence—your house, your clothes, your car. But then again, I'm obsessive when it comes to cleanliness. Leslie, our youngest cheese maker, says that Consider Bardwell Farm is the cleanest farm she's ever seen. The pens are raked and covered with fresh bedding several times a week. The milking parlor is swept of any dirt and debris after each milking. And no one is allowed to enter the cheese-making area without removing their shoes and putting on clogs that we keep just inside the door in a variety of sizes and never leave that area.

Somehow space was found for my boys in the back of the farmer's truck. The only consolation I could take was that Betsy seemed very pleasant and compassionate. I realized too late that they still had their white temporary identification collars on, and as I drove away I worried that I'd failed in my last responsibility, which was to remove the collars so they wouldn't become entangled in other goats' legs. That's superneurotic me: I'm sending them away to become meat, yet I couldn't sleep that night because I left their collars on.

The most valuable aspect of that trip to Shaftsbury wasn't the few dollars I received for my young bucks. (The farmer paid me five dollars each.) Rather, it was the advice on pulling newborn goats that I received from the Lawrences. They told me that they let their babies stay on their mothers, but just for an hour or so, long enough for the moms to lick their faces clean. (The babies are born completely covered in amniotic fluid, and the mothers know instinctively that they must clean the nose and mouth to help them breathe.) The Lawrences mentioned a New Zealand study that found that when goats were pulled immediately from their moms and kissed, and breathed on by humans, they didn't grow up to be as healthy because their rumens developed human microbes. Those licked by their own mothers, instead, were exposed to goat microbes, which enabled their rumens to digest food better. The Lawrences added that allowing the does to indulge their maternal instincts also soothes them, and it reduces the farmhands' workload: They would have to clean up each baby right away, which is tough when delivering multiple babies at the same time.

I was glad to hear about the face-licking practice. I respected the Lawrences and their dedication to raising dairy goats. This news suggested that there was a happy medium between leaving the babies on their mothers so long that they become a management problem after separation and pulling the kids off their mothers immediately.

Despite asserting my authority to the farmhands, I do realize that there is always more to learn about this business and its subtleties, about how each season brings new situations and challenges. In the same way that crop farmers know that no two springs or summers are alike, that nature continually throws you curves, so it is in animal husbandry. Just when you think you know every disease, parasite, and condition a goat can have, something new comes along. (But I try to stay on top of any issues; I even bought a microscope to examine parasites and eggs on fecal samples. Over the long haul, this can save hundreds of dollars in veterinarian lab fees. I also had a hunch that I'd hit a new milestone when I felt pride, even pleasure, in running behind a goat and letting poop drop into my gloved hand.) So much for being a dilettante.

I WAS ABLE TO IMPLEMENT THE LAWRENCES' ADVICE WITH THE majority of the herd, beginning as soon as I got back to the farm because another goat was going into labor.

This time it was Pearl—as in Black Pearl, because of her luxurious black coat. Labor can last several hours in first-time moms. But Pearl had a giant boy the previous year and seemed to need little help delivering her babies. Goats in general deliver babies with a restrained dignity that seems to put many of their human counterparts to shame. No epidurals here.

Pearl's labor produced both a girl and a boy. We planned to follow the Lawrences' suggestion to leave Pearl's babies on her for one hour—until another goat, Samara, who'd given birth the day before, suddenly tried to kidnap one of Pearl's babies and was starting to lick it. We had never seen a kidnapping in progress before and stopped it immediately.

There was a simple explanation for Samara's behavior: New mothers' hormones and deep-seated instincts tell them that they should be caring for a baby. Heeding the call of nature, they will kidnap and adopt if necessary. In the coming days, the plaintive cries of mothers trying to locate babies would be a familiar one in the barn. In Pearl's case, she spent a couple of days outside the barn, standing by the window nearest to where she had given birth, calling to her missing kids and waiting for a reply.

IF THE DOE IS STRUGGLING, YOU MAY HAVE TO LEND A hand, literally. You put on a clean rubber glove, wash your hands and the goat's hind end with betadine solution, lubricate the glove with K-Y Jelly, insert it into the birth canal, and sort out the baby's head and legs so they "present" (come out) in the proper position. During a difficult presentation, you may even have to pull the baby out yourself, as Laura did with the first of California's triplets, delivered at around 5 P.M. behind the barn on a beautiful day—the twelve-pounder was followed by an eight-pounder and a four-pounder. Ultimately, they emerged from their mother's womb without complications. (Multiple births are common among goats, generally with the first baby being the most robust and the smallest the least likely to flourish without human intervention, not only because of their small size but also because goats, like humans, have just two teats.)

Kids are supposed to come out front feet first, followed by the nose and head. When Lailani gave birth this year, the third of her triplets, unlike California's kids, was presenting itself ass backwards—that is, with its ass forward. His body was bent double with his head pressed against his butt. Or as Debbie put it in her inimitable fashion, "He was wearing his butt as a hat." Laura, who tried to deliver him first, had been able to locate the neck, but not the head. In a goat, this is a breech birth, and it's potentially catastrophic; if the amniotic sac breaks before the baby's head is out, the little one can suffocate.

When Debbie reached inside the goat to locate the baby's head, she looked as though she'd gone into a trance, gazing up at the sky. All the while, Lailani was screaming. But Debbie somehow turned the baby and extracted him. Debbie saved two lives that day, Lailani's and the baby's, and she was our hero.

A while after a goat has finished pushing out the baby, she expels the placenta. It's not uncommon for her to eat it. While the notion might disgust humans, it's incredibly nourishing and it's also a survival instinct on her baby's behalf: In the wild, they leave little evidence behind for predators to signal that there's a helpless baby around.

Perhaps the most important accessory in the birthing process is clean towels. I put out an all-points-bulletin to friends and neighbors before the start of each kidding season, saying that we'll take all old, fraying towels (which I then clean). We use those towels in many ways. When a new baby kid is ready to fall out of its mother (or dam), we rush to cushion the fall with a clean towel. That also prevents the newborn from landing on a soiled bed pack. Then after a mom licks the guck off her baby and leaves it spanking clean, the baby is wet. Since the barn in April is probably 40°F and often colder, we towel-dry the infant goat and even use a hairdryer—gently and at low temperature. Towels are also crucial for cleaning up the mom's nether parts.

In most cases, the umbilical cord breaks by itself, and the mother cleans the area thoroughly. Many goat dairy farmers also dip the umbilical cord in extra strength iodine, then tie it off with soft string and cut it with sharp scissors two or three inches from the kid's body. If the mother has done a good job cleaning, then we don't bother tying the cord, but we do use the iodine dip for good measure.

After putting the kids in a special sanitary pen reserved for the newborns, we return our attention to the moms. They expend a tremendous amount of energy during the birthing process, so we offer them a bucket of warm water laced with molasses along with a little grain to help them recharge their batteries.

THE KIDDING SEASON LASTED TWO MONTHS. WHEN THE dust settled, the dams had given birth to twenty-four sets of twins, six sets of triplets, and fifteen singles. Of those, thirty-seven were girls and forty-four were boys. The grand total was eighty-one baby goats.

Whenever I worry about the decisions I've made or hear the heartbreaking cries of mothers after I've pulled their newborns away, I come back to something Melvin Lawrence told me when I recounted the turmoil over Lailani's labor. "They're working mothers," Melvin stated matter-of-factly. And it's just that simple.

They're not pets. They're not meat goats (except the boys). They exist to provide as much high-quality milk as possible that can be turned into cheese. We do everything possible to make their lives comfortable and happy. And there are worse things in the world than free room and board, universal health care, and a view of Vermont out your barnyard window.

The last goat to give birth, or so we thought, was Peony on April 25.

It was a baby boy, whom we baptized Peabody. Laura cuddled and cooed over him for days before returning to Texas and her real life as an optometrist. She made me promise to treat her last-born with great devotion.

But to our surprise, Peabody was not the final baby of the herd. Over two months later, on July 9, two of our farmhands, big Corey and little Corey, as I call them—ages twenty-one and thirteen—were checking the goats, as they do first thing every morning, to make sure everybody is safe, healthy, and staying out of mischief. They crossed the road to where we pasture our yearlings and spotted a beautiful black baby girl standing beside Dawn: the eighty-second baby. By the time the boys found her, Dawn had already licked the baby clean, and by the end of her first day, the infant was climbing the Stairway to Heaven on her own, following the example of her three-month-old classmates.

It's funny how the deluge of April babies is always so stressful and we can't wait for kidding season to be over, and yet the arrival of a beautiful little baby girl later, much later, in the season is a cause for celebration at the farm. That day everyone greeted me with the good news of the birth when I returned from the city. We hadn't thought Dawn had been bred, because pregnant does usually become very wide and develop an udder. Dawn did neither. We also didn't know who the sire was, because we never saw the telltale colored-crayon marking on Dawn's haunch, which would indicate that she was bred to a specific buck. It could have been Boris or perhaps Kennedy.

Dawn is the typical light brown color of the Oberhasli breed, but her mother, Midnight, is black. (Hence the themed day-to-night names.) Grandma's color gene had apparently skipped a generation, so in consideration of both mom and grandma, we named the baby Moonlight.

With Moonlight, we were able again to observe the difference between leaving babies on their mothers, as we had with our 2007 kids, or pulling them off. Moonlight was the only kid of the 2008 class we let stay with her mother. She was so far behind and so much smaller than the rest that I decided she needed all the help and protection she could get. And truth be told, we'd just been through raising eighty-one babies, and no one wanted to bottle-feed another little one every four hours.

Dawn more than fulfilled her maternal obligations. To help Moonlight get socialized and run with the herd as quickly as possible, I put both mother and daughter in the kids' pen. Dawn had her hooves full trying to protect her precious little one from Moonlight's comparatively streetwise eight- to twelve-week-old companions. It was amusing to watch: Dawn would head-butt any kid she thought was infringing on Moonlight's personal space, which was just about everybody, since Moonlight seemed to have no fear of being right in the mix.

Like most kids, Moonlight had a problem with authority. One hot August afternoon, Dawn stood in the shade bleating for Moonlight to join her. But the baby ignored her call. She was curious about the humans approaching; I was bringing some visitors to the pen to show her off. But even though she disobeyed her mom, we have noticed over time that she acts much more aloof around humans than the other kids of 2008, because her first and strongest bond was with her mother.

FIVE

milk maids

THE HEARTBREAK OF SEPARATING BABIES FROM THEIR
mothers—my anguish and theirs—subsided after a few days,
with the babies transferring their affection to their human handlers and fellow kids (you haven't experienced *cute* until you've
seen the way they pile on top of one another for warmth when
sleeping in the cardboard box they call home the first few days
of their life), and the mothers returning to the reassuring routine of farm life: reporting to the barn early each morning to be
milked, grazing all day, then returning to be milked in the
evening.

The mothers start producing milk, or "freshening," as it's
called, in April, when they have their babies. Our farm doesn't hit

full milk production until mid-May, when all the goats (with the exception of surprises such as Moonlight) have had their kids.

Anyone who thinks of goats as unsophisticated, even dumb, creatures with indistinguishable personalities would think differently after watching the way they negotiate their proper place on the milking line—or head-butt when negotiation fails. The social structure of the herd is impressively complex and nuanced. I've mentioned my special relationship with Koko, but in fact every goat is unique, the result of nature and nurture, genes and environment.

Take Petunia, for instance, one of our six original goats, who is unfortunately no longer with us. She was not the friendliest animal on the farm. In fact, she was downright ornery. The girl had a short fuse. Once she pulled the vet's cap off and yanked out some hair. She would turn around and nip you if you walked behind her. It didn't hurt because goats don't have upper teeth, but it certainly got your attention.

At one point, I called the New Hampshire woman who'd sold me Petunia and asked whether she could offer any insight into the goat's problematic personality. She explained that Petunia was the runt of the litter and had gotten used to being last in line. She knew her place and felt secure there. And, as absurd as it sounds, she wasn't going to let anyone take it away from her.

But the others also seem to have their own social strategies to make. It's like watching high schoolers in the lunchroom. As the girls enter the milking parlor in several rotations, there's a lead goat at the front of each group, the same one every time

(Magnolia in the first rotation, Iris in the second—ironically, daughter and mother). Less dominant does dutifully fall in behind, and the smallest, youngest, and weakest goats, such as Lailani and Petunia, bring up the rear.

Within the hierarchy, there are particular goats who exhibit idiosyncratic behavior. Iris and her daughter Magnolia are good examples. The two are inseparable. Although all mothers and daughters bond, these two do virtually everything together: graze, milk, sleep. They're also two of the biggest, heartiest eaters in the herd. Pity the poor goat who finds herself wedged between these two bruisers at the hay feeder.

Then there's Koko. When the goats are being milked, they feed on molasses-coated grain pellets to keep them busy and happy. After one shift of goats is milked and shooed out of the milking parlor, most goats return to the pen without complaint to munch on good hay, which will supply much-needed fiber to their rumens. Not Koko. She enjoys hanging out. She'll start down the ramp, then stop dead in her tracks and loiter there. Sometimes she'll turn around and try to head back up, perhaps thinking her charm and good looks will persuade me to give her an extra serving of grain. (They don't.) But when admonishments don't work, Koko sometimes has to be taken literally by the collar, led down the ramp, and put back in the pen. She doesn't take it personally. To her, it's a game; I think she does it for the attention as much as anything else. No matter how much you scold, she'll try her luck again the next time she's milked.

Koko's antics notwithstanding, the milking routine usually

goes like this: The girls are herded into the barn (though in fact they require little prodding, given the allure of those sweet grain treats; rather, they fall obediently in line and file into the milking parlor holding pen). There they patiently await their group's turn. When the time comes, they barrel through the gate and gallop up the ramp to the milking parlor and over to one of the fourteen milking stations.

There's a certain amount of pushing and shoving to get to the grain, located in troughs that run the length of the milking room. In their excitement, some goats insert their heads between the stanchions rather than through them and need help getting out. Then, whoever has the milking honors, be it Alex Eaton, Minny Buley, Amber Goff, or me, goes around and hand-milks the first three squirts from each teat into a metal "strip cup," so called because you're stripping the first milk out of the teat. Each cup has a screen that will catch any milk abnormalities that might indicate a mastitis infection. Next, we dip each teat into a plastic cup filled with a disinfecting iodine-water solution, leave it on for a minimum of thirty seconds, and finally wipe the teat off with a separate paper towel for each side. Only when the teats are completely disinfected and wiped dry do we attach a milking inflation unit to each one. An inflation is essentially a pulsating, elongated suction cup that mimics the sucking rhythm of a baby goat and is attached to a hose. Milking out the goat takes about two minutes. When finished, we use a stronger iodine solution to do the "post dip," which keeps the teat opening bacteria-free until it closes naturally. Dan Scruton, of the Vermont Agency of Agriculture and an authority on milking procedures, once conducted a milking workshop at our farm. He cautioned against leaving dirty bedding, allowing lactating goats to loaf in wet, muddy areas, and using anything but pristinely sanitary inflations, lest the teat become exposed to bacterial infections, which lurk in every barn and farm area. He stressed that healthy teats are a dairy farm's most valuable asset.

It's loud in the parlor because of the vacuum pump that sends milk from the pulsating inflations on the goat's udder to an overhead pipe that runs into the adjoining room, where the farm's large, refrigerated 300-gallon bulk tank is located. The milk sits in the tank—by law no longer than seventy-two hours—until it is pumped into the heated cheese vat in the cheese-making room.

The cheese making and milking revolve around the goats' lactation cycle. The amount of milk a dairy goat produces varies in part according to the time of year and where she is in her annual kidding cycle. The does produce the maximum amount of milk in the first two months after giving birth. That parallels their behavior in nature, where babies are nursed by their mothers for two months, then weaned. At that point, a mother goat would naturally stop producing milk. But in the dairy, the animals continue to produce milk because we continue to stimulate their mammary glands; however, it's only about three-quarters of what they produced earlier in their cycle. By the time they're bred in November, that's dropped to half the amount of peak production. The does are then "dried off" in December—that is, we gradually stop milking them. At the same time, we also stop giving them grain; for a week, we milk only once a day, and then we milk every other day. Without the extra protein from the grain and the stimulation of being milked, a goat will stop producing after a couple of weeks. For the next three and a half months, the pregnant goats get to loaf and rest. When they kid in the spring, the milk starts to flow again.

The annual cycle is only part of the story. Milk production is also affected by what the goats are grazing on. The composition of pasture plants and grasses changes from month to month. In the spring and early summer, the grass grows fast because the weather is wet. Because it also contains more moisture, the grass contributes to making the goats produce a greater quantity of milk, along with the natural spike in postpartum milk production. During those months, the water content of the milk is high and the protein and fat content are low.

The most nutritious grasses are the late-season grasses, grown in September. The hay that's made from them is known as "rowen hay," an old Yankee term. Those grasses have grown more slowly because it's not as hot, and thus they have more stock, more substance, to them. This is probably their second or even third regrowth, since the goats have grazed on them or they've previously been cut for hay. The more times the grass is grazed, the more nutrients will be concentrated in the regrowth.

The wonderful thing about Vermont is that we traditionally get a fair amount of rain in September, so the grass is still growing strong. Farmers in drier locales have to be careful how they rotate goats through their pastures, because conditions can become almost drought-like in late summer and early fall. Normally, not in Vermont.

Our cheese-making schedule follows the milk cycle. You'd think that fall would be a bad time for cheese making, since milk production has declined significantly by then. But it's actually an ideal period. There's less milk, but it's better milk for making cheese. Late in the season, there's more protein and fat, more "solids" in the milk. In fact, the fat and protein content is probably twenty percent higher than in May or June. For that reason, there's a higher cheese yield from less milk.

We reserve some of that nutritious late-season hay for the following spring, when the goats are making babies, producing milk, and expending lots of energy. When goats, cows, or any ruminants are not being milked, they need less protein in their diet. Therefore, we feed them the less rich, early-season hay during January, February, and March when they're dried off and are just lounging around the barn, waiting for their babies to be born.

PART OF WHAT MAKES OUR CHEESE MAKER PETER DIXON such a master is that he's closely attuned to the goats' lactation cycle and knows how to "read" the milk. He creates a basic process for making each type of cheese, but then makes adjustments for the real milk composition at different stages of the cycle.

Peter is also aware of how specific pastures might affect the milk. There's a spirited debate in the industry about whether "terroir" matters in cheese. The term is borrowed from the wine world, where it refers to the specific elements of place—soil composition, drainage, sun exposure, and climate—that can ultimately be reflected in a glass of wine.

Peter believes it makes a difference in cheese, too. According to him, weather and soil have a definite effect on the character of cheese, and both weather and soil differ dramatically from one part of Vermont to the next. In other words, the cheese made at our farm would taste slightly different from cheese made with the exact same methods at a farm one hour away. That's because the goats are grazing on our grasses, which have their own unique composition and mineral content, based on the microclimate and underlying soil of our property. We run soil tests each spring to make sure the soil is rich and has balanced nutrients.

Peter makes his point by comparing our Mettowee, a fresh farmstead goat's milk cheese, to an equivalent cheese made at Blue Ledge Farm, a goat cheese creamery near Middlebury, about sixty miles to the north. (The reason to compare fresh rather than aged cheeses is because they're so straightforward. Without aging, there's no contribution of the rind to the flavor; it's a very direct taste comparison.) Peter contends that he can taste the difference between their cheese and ours. Both are excellent cheeses, but our Mettowee is moister and less acidic.

Thinking about terroir, I used to worry that the sulfuric flavor of our water might affect our cheese in some way. Luckily, it doesn't seem to at all. Either that, or it makes for great-tasting cheese. Sulfur is present in the slate bedrock in this part of Vermont. In the nineteenth century, sulfur-spring spas were the places to be cured of many ills. Nearby Saratoga Springs, New York, about forty miles west of the farm, still welcomes vacationers to its celebrated sulfur baths.

At home, however, the rotten-egg smell that occasionally comes from our faucets can detract from the pleasure of brushing your teeth. We use only bottled spring water in the house; the Pellegrino we serve at dinner isn't an affectation, it's a matter of protecting the taste buds.

Although sulfur dissipates when exposed to air for a few hours, it is obviously in the water the goats drink, and cheese is forty percent water. But its bouquet has been infused with the taste of fresh grasses from the green hills and burbling brooks. At least, that's my story and I'm sticking to it.

IF TERROIR IS STILL A SCIENTIFIC PUZZLE, THAT'S NOT THE case with much else that goes on at a dairy farm. The Vermont Dairy Herd Improvement Association comes to meter, measure, and analyze each goat's milk production every month. Bill Haggerty, a neighbor and DHIA employee, arrives at 6 A.M. and attaches meters to each goat's milk hose, which allows him to determine how much milk each individual is producing. He also takes a milk sample back to the lab, and the DHIA analyzes it. The monthly reports are crucial in helping us evaluate how profitable each goat is for the farm.

The DHIA's monthly report indicates the number of days every individual goat has been "in milk" as well as the milk's fat and protein content. But the dairy association also provides us with a "hot sheet" the day after they meter. These data include each goat's somatic (white blood cell) count. A very high count would indicate that the animal might have an udder infection. If so, it would have to be tested for mastitis, an infection in the mammary gland, and possibly prescribed antibiotics. It's illegal to mix antibiotic-infused milk with milk from healthy goats, so we would have to hand-milk treated goats and discard the milk for a number of days specified by the USDA.

I am still amazed and impressed by how much testing we do on each animal. Peter takes bulk-tank samples every week to be tested for bacteria and somatic counts on the whole herd's milk output. He is protecting the integrity of raw-milk cheese making, so that no harmful pathogens enter the cheeses. Every other month at least, I take left- and right-udder samples from each goat and have them analyzed by a lab at Cornell University to ensure that no toxic bacteria are developing. Also, Greg Lockwood, our Vermont Agency of Agriculture cheese inspector, appears suddenly and without warning in our driveway once a month—usually before dawn—to take a sample from our bulk tank for analysis of the milk components and to make sure there are no antibiotics in the milk.

Most Vermont cheese farmers put their livestock, milk, and cheese through similarly rigorous protocols, particularly because there has been a lot of controversy lately about the health and safety of the U.S. food supply. But from our perspective, there's no question that our goats receive more frequent checkups than the human locavores who produce and eat the cheese. And this, of course, is one of the best reasons to buy cheese from highly scrutinized creameries.

All this testing is not only important for safety, but it also helps us know our goats better. According to our May 2008 DHIA hot sheet, Nadia was our star, producing 14.7 pounds of milk on May 20, the day the data were collected. The following month that honor went to Savannah. Good news for me was that Lailani, even though older and weaker than many, was right in the game in terms of production.

I've taken a lot of grief for keeping Lailani. People say, "Why would you want to keep a goat that's always having health problems, that may be passing along bad genes?" Her impressive milk-producing capability is part of the explanation. But I also love her, as unprofessional as that may sound. She is from excellent stock, and I couldn't imagine not taking care of her until her last breath.

Also, having a closed herd, I don't buy new stock. After Lailani's difficult delivery—difficult for both her and me, considering the grief I got—she seemed to be on the rebound. She was gaining weight, the sheen had returned to her coat, and she was moving faster. Often, in fact, she was no longer the last goat to enter the milking parlor. She wasn't exactly head-butting Magnolia, one of the most dominant does, or Iris to be first in line, but she remained a productive member of the herd.

what west pawlet
needs is a café

IN JUNE AT THE FARM, THERE'S NO REST FOR THE WEARY.
By five o'clock one weekend morning, I'd already downed several cups of coffee and was hoisting a heavy bale of hay to carry
it out to the barnyard for the goats' breakfast. Our guest that
weekend told me later that after being awakened—probably by
our rooster—she'd turned over to go back to sleep, then happened to glance out the window and spot my burdened form.
Until that moment, she hadn't appreciated the enormity—she
might have been thinking insanity—of the responsibility I'd un-
dertaken. Frankly, sometimes I can't fathom it myself: the financial, psychological, and, perhaps most of all, physical toll.

I didn't envision it this way when we started. The enterprise grew slowly, but it became virtually all-consuming. There was no grand plan. I wasn't like one of those hedge-fund guys who had made a fortune bundling subprime mortgages or collateralized debt obligations—or whatever it is they do—and then decided to turn their master-of-the-universe ways to raising goats, sheep, or grass-fed beef. They envision that they can buy a few hundred acres, quickly build their dream house and matching barns, "outsource" a team to make prize-winning goat cheese, trendy yogurt, or cuts of porterhouse laden with healthy omega-3s from their organically fertilized fields, and watch the money roll in. At some point—usually sooner than later—they discover that making money on Wall Street is a breeze compared to turning a profit on a farm.

At least we started slow. We didn't have grandiose financial ambitions. You could not have accused us of hubris back in 2001 when we bought the farm and my loftiest goal was learning how to ski moguls. As a matter of fact, my first commercial venture in Vermont was a café. I realize only in retrospect that this was a dry run, an experiment to convince myself that I was capable of managing a retail business where I was dealing directly with customers.

The idea for a café came to me in the fall of 2002. I'd been attending a business extension course on women in agriculture at the University of Vermont. Coming home from class one particularly bleak Saturday afternoon, I drove through our forlorn little village of West Pawlet. My entrepreneurial gene activated, I got to thinking that what this sleepy town needed was a café, a place where the community could gather. The village is little more than a crossroads with a yield sign, containing only a general store called Dutchies, a post office, and several empty storefronts. West Pawlet had peaked somewhere in the late nineteenth century, and not much had improved since an 1896 fire burned down whole swaths of the town.

Driving through the village, I suddenly imagined one of those abandoned storefronts as the site of a new café. I could visualize its painted facade, its multicolored flowers in window boxes, its excellent selection of teas and baked goods—and me in the middle of it, helping bring the town back to life. (I suspect I was reading too much magic realism at the time.)

This was also a period in my life as a literary agent when I was working with a lot of chefs. I got to see how their restaurants operated (or business empires, in some cases) and observe the passion, creativity, and sweat equity they brought to cuisine. I was audacious enough to think I shared some of those qualities. I had competitiveness, perfectionism, and workaholism all lined up—but not culinary genius, unfortunately (though I did know my way around a kitchen).

Within a few days, I dropped by the West Pawlet post office and asked the postmistress, Sylvia Kramer, for the names of the owners of three empty storefronts on the main street. The first two didn't respond when I tried to contact them, but the third, the West Pawlet Fish and Game Club, did.

By that time, the club was an organization in name only, at least judging by the leaky roof and the decades of dust that had accumulated inside its clubhouse. But in January 2003, the eight honorable club members agreed to let me have it rent-free. The next month, I started scrubbing and kept it up every Saturday and Sunday that winter in the freezing cold.

Rust, who knows something about renovation, tried to warn me off. "You don't have any idea what you're getting into," he grumbled. "Do you really have the money for this? It's going to cost a lot." I just kept saying, "Don't worry."

Pursuing my fantasy, I gave the club's facade a fresh coat of apple-green paint and added window boxes filled with vinca, geraniums, and daisies. (Facing north, they all died within two weeks.) Two apple-green benches were placed in front of the café for customers who preferred to sit outside and enjoy the fresh air.

Inside, it was a modest-sized hall with fake wood paneling and a kitchen. Fortunately, it came decorated; I decided to keep the trophies from the Fish and Game Club's proud past: mounted deer and moose heads, a stuffed snowy owl, and rugs made from Holstein cow hides.

I painted the plywood bingo tables bright yellow and hung a few paintings, some by Roy Egg, an artist whose studio was just beyond Dutchies, located in an attention-getting house painted like a red-and-white checkerboard à la Grandma Moses. Roy specializes in wildlife paintings and farm-animal portraits and cutouts. His work is popular in these parts, occupying many a windowsill and fireplace mantel in West Pawlet and surrounding towns.

The café's lamps were assembled from entangled driftwood branches and embellished with lampshades by Judy Lake, a Pawlet lampshade maker and author of *The Lampshade Lady's Guide to Lighting Up Your Life,* a book I agented. The shades were decorated with vintage red French fabric; one also had a Grandma Moses design.

THE WEST PAWLET FISH AND GAME CAFÉ OPENED ON Memorial Day 2003. Before our big debut, Roy Egg, being a savvy artist, contacted his friend Mark Frost, who owns *The Chronicle* in Glens Falls, New York. Mark came over, took some photographs, and wrote an article for the newspaper. On opening day, there were lines of people from Glens Falls, mostly carloads of retired ladies looking for foodie action.

The real Vermonters in West Pawlet were supportive in their own way, though I'm not sure whether that was because they thought I was providing a service to the community or because I let them hunt on our property. They weren't about to spend $2 on a scone, and they probably didn't fully appreciate how unusual it was to find French rose tea in this corner of Vermont's Indian River Valley. But they would buy a cup of coffee and hang out and they liked the souvenir Fish and Game Club buttons and honorary membership cards I had made.

For the two summers that I ran the West Pawlet Fish and Game Café, I even dressed up, at least compared to my normal state of hay- and dung-flecked disrepair on the farm. I would don a hip apron from the Anthropologie boutique in Manhattan, brush on some lipstick, and greet guests at the door. (Before and after my café years, I'd wake up and decide which of my "rags" to wear that day. That's how I referred to my clothes: rags. Ever since buying the farm, I've been wearing only secondhand clothes. The Manhattan consignment shop Housing Works is now my mecca for farm and office wear. My Prada bags cost about $15 these days.)

Despite the café's distinctive decoration, *Architectural Digest* wasn't banging down the door to shoot a photo spread. But we did get a visit from Susan Sargent, a local designer and wife of Tom Peters, coauthor of the eighties bestseller *In Search of Excellence*. She stopped by for coffee one Saturday morning and politely offered to sell me some of her amazing, colorful fabrics to brighten up the place. I had been using Indian bedspreads from Urban Outfitters to cover the big tables and to supply atmosphere. I couldn't take Susan up on her offer because I had no money to invest in anything upscale. If I grossed $300 on a weekend, I considered myself rolling in dough. The eclectic decor remained one of the café's charms.

In addition to being owner and hostess, I also made all the baked goods for the café. After an intensive workweek in Manhattan, I'd come to Vermont to bake all day on Friday, then rise at 5 A.M. on Saturday to do last-minute baking and whip some fresh cream to dollop on the scones, fruit tarts, and quick breads. I was hauling teas from Fauchon, a Parisian luxury-food shop with an outpost on Park Avenue, as well as bringing in exotic coffees from McNulty's Tea & Coffee Co. on Christopher Street in the West Village.

Scones were my signature dish, but my raspberry tart was also quite popular. Once I made one with the assistance of Pascal Vittu, at the time the cheese buyer at restaurant Daniel, a *New York Times* four-star dining destination in Manhattan. He was visiting the farm with his wife and stepdaughter and helped me pick the raspberries. Pascal insisted on hand-cleaning every raspberry with a wet cloth, then drying every little segment. He watched as I served the tarts; I dare not imagine his thoughts. The West Pawlet Fish and Game Café was a bit more primitive than restaurant Daniel.

Every day, I'd stash our earnings into a cash box. By the end of the first summer, I had made almost $5,000. I had no idea whether that exceeded expenses, and frankly I didn't care. I was having a ball. I was meeting many new people and enjoying the fact that they seemed to be responding positively to this new hangout—one I'd made from scratch. My bubbly English friend, Philippa Katz, dubbed it the Café Voltaire.

At times, I felt like the friendly neighborhood bartender. People would come in early so they could tell me what woeful things were happening in their lives. I discovered that there are a lot of lonely people in Vermont longing for company.

The café's regulars included Jimmy Stearns, one of my favorite neighbors, who had recently become single after a long marriage. He would get his coffee and a piece of pie, then sit in the back by himself, watching the human comedy unfold. He had quite a sweet tooth, and I was always grateful for the compliments he showered on my baking skills.

Then there was Pastor Joe, the local Baptist minister, who confided his liberal leanings to me, even though he didn't dare share them with his conservative congregation. I knew the café and I had been accepted the Sunday I looked out the window to see Pastor Joe leading his aged flock down the hill from his church to our apple-green café. Fortunately, he'd warned me in advance, so we could guarantee that there'd still be baked goods left at 11 A.M., when the service ended. In their honor, I'd whipped up a menu of religiously themed goods: divinity fudge, devil's food cake, angel food cake, and other sugary after-church rewards.

Another habitué was George Bouret, a professional photographer. He had moved to the area two years earlier after his wife, Carol, a pretty woman with long red hair, graduated from veterinary school and took a job at the Granville Veterinary Service a few miles away. But a couple of months before the café opened, Carol had died. George came every weekend and even lent a helping hand when things got chaotic. Since he knew almost everyone, he acted as my patron, introducing me to customers and easing the way for me.

Not all our patrons were so enchanting. We also attracted a weirdo in his twenties who lived around the corner and didn't confine his visits to business hours. He'd walk through the back door before the opening bell, wearing combat boots and lots of chains. Perhaps they were dog chains, seeing how he kept guard dogs at his house. Eventually the cops took him away after he pulled a gun on someone at Dutchies. His presence was a reminder that Vermont's wholesome Ben & Jerry's image tells only part of the story.

Rust also came often. Although he was initially apprehensive about the expense of the café, he eventually embraced the idea. He'd sashay in around 11 A.M. and have a cup of tea. If we had houseguests, they'd drop by too, though whether it was out of support or morbid curiosity, I'm not certain.

I ran the West Pawlet Fish and Game Café from 8 A.M. to 1 P.M. on Saturdays and Sundays throughout the summers of 2003 and 2004. Within a few months, the café's reputation had spread (though there wasn't much competition), and my selection of teas, baked goods, and reading copies of the Sunday *New York Times* started attracting as many weekenders as locals. On one particularly slow Sunday, Rust noticed four bicyclists outside the café and hailed them down. He convinced them to come inside for some refreshments (read: to spend money). The group was led by Tom and Sally Birchard. As it turned out, Tom owns a legendary hipster hangout and eatery on the Lower East Side of Manhattan called Veselka. Sally is a veterinarian. It was Tom's birthday, and I just happened to have a gorgeous, unsliced raspberry tart. I rigged it up with a candle, and we all sang "Happy Birthday." Tom and I immediately began talking about a Veselka cookbook; eventually, I made a deal for *The Veselka Cookbook* and we got it published. Talk about synergy.

BY THE SUMMER OF 2005, I COULDN'T KEEP ALL THE PLATES spinning: the literary agency, the café, the dairy farm, and by that point the fledgling cheese-making business. So I gave the café operation to two young mothers, both recent graduates of Green Mountain College. But when they realized what a nightmarish, relentless workload the café required, they quietly closed it down after one short season.

It may sound crazy, but even now, five years later, I hope eventually to resurrect the café. I like giving parties, and running the café was like throwing a party every weekend.

But its greatest virtue was that it helped introduce us and our farm to the community. When we started making cheese in 2003, I held tastings at the café. I'd augment our chèvre with a selection of cheeses from Murray's Cheese, a shop in Manhattan, and type up little signs describing their flavor notes, wine pairings, cooking ideas, etc. We charged $5 per person. It was extraordinary how well customers responded; there are a surprising number of sophisticated palates in this tiny, rural community. All combined, the enterprise helped convince the town stalwarts that we weren't softheaded weekenders who planned to move on as soon as we lost interest—or lost too much money. Consider Bardwell Farm wasn't going anywhere. We intended to make the farm as integral to the community as it had been a hundred years earlier.

SEVEN

chasing the
cheese maker

I HAD ORIGINALLY ASSUMED THAT I WOULD RAISE SHEEP.
It appealed to the Anglophile in me and, of course, to Rust. I
even attended an American Sheep Dairy Conference at Cornell
University in 2002, one of several animal husbandry seminars
I attended early on to help bring me up to speed as a farmer. Although Rust simply liked the imagined view of little white wooly
animals dotting our distant pastures, my interest was a more
commercial one. I was a businessperson and the idea of making
the farm and cheese business viable had become more real to
me. I knew that sheep's milk sold for ninety-two cents a pound,
while cow's milk went for twenty cents a pound and goat's milk
for forty cents a pound. And sheep's milk cheese was a lot rarer;

to this day, there are many more goat and cow's milk cheese makers than sheep's milk cheese makers in Vermont and neighboring New York State. It seemed as if there was more opportunity in sheep. At the time, The Old Chatham Sheepherding Company was the rising star. I wanted some of that market share.

I switched to goats largely because of Marie Louise Ryan, our first employee, who started working with us in May 2003. I'd found her through a University of Vermont website that connects farmers with people looking for farm jobs. Also, I'd seen a thousand sheep walk off a cliff in the film *Far from the Madding Crowd*. If I was going to be surrounded by animals, I at least wanted them to be intelligent and curious, which Marie Louise assured me goats were. We called Marie Louise our "French" helper, even though she was from New Orleans. But she'd spent five years in Provence making cheese. Her ambition was eventually to start her own goat cheese–making farm in Vermont.

It was she who selected our Oberhasli breed, picking that because it was the same breed she had herded and milked in Provence. They're one of the top three milk producers, after French Alpines and Saanens, and much rarer in the United States than the others. Nubians, which produce less milk but whose butterfat content is higher, are the most popular in the United States.

I'm now a big booster of goats, although I know that they have something of an image problem, especially compared to sheep, which seem so fuzzy and benign. No one counts goats when going to sleep.

It's true that a goat will munch on the occasional dog-food can or your Star Magnolia, but that's only because they're curious animals. They're actually somewhat picky eaters.

I suspect that our vet, Dr. Amanda Alderink, shares my preference for goats over sheep, though she could never openly say so, for fear of alienating her sheep-farm clients. If she's like me, she finds goats more intellectually stimulating. She has told me that sheep are very herd driven. You definitely see more independence with goats. In her view, goats are quirkier and more personality driven.

Sheep farmers would undoubtedly take issue with that. Among the sheep partisans in my neighborhood are Philippa Katz, one of my best friends, who has a sheep farm just across the border in New York State. Pippa, as we call her, claims her sheep have distinct personalities. When they don't want to follow her border collie's orders, they've been known to stamp their feet in protest. Their ram, on the other hand, has the manners of an Oxford-educated gentleman, according to Pippa (a Brit herself). "He's very polite," she said of his mating dance, which is more like a stroll. "He goes around and chats with the ewes. He introduces himself—'Hello, ladies!'—and shoots the breeze a little bit. Everybody's happy at the end of the day. They sit around him in a little circle."

I'll still throw in my lot with goats. You don't need border collies to herd them because they follow routines once they learn them. The only time they get confused is if humans are dumb enough to leave an important gate open that they're used to having closed, and they follow this new path—in my case, onto the road. However, I believe that it's their intelligence and curiosity that compels them to run through that gate in the first place to explore the outside world. Then they panic. I imagine they wonder: Are we on water? Or is it a cloud? Where shall we go? What shall we do? Fortunately, if you calmly put a little grain in a bucket and shake it, they'll follow you back to safety.

WE TOOK OUR FIRST STAB AT CHEESE MAKING IN AUGUST 2003 (while the café was in full swing) after Marie Louise and I picked up our first six goats in New Hampshire and transported them back to Vermont. Marie Louise was in fact the reason I finally decided to buy animals at that point, even though I had my hands full with the café and was still working in the city all week. She had given me the impression that she was going to assume full responsibility for their care—or that was my fantasy. I'd even asked her point-blank as we drove to pick them up, "Do you have any idea what you're getting yourself into?"

Marie Louise's first assignment had been to prepare the barn. This beautiful, massive structure is known as a "bank barn" because it's built into the side of an embankment. The goats live on the first floor, which also contains all the rooms related to the cheese-making operation: the milking parlor, the cheese-making room, and the caves. On the second floor is a giant hayloft or haymow, as our farmhands call it, which is filled every summer with fragrant, freshly cut hay. Adjoining the barn are two towering silos, which are now empty. Like most farmers these days, we no longer use them to store grain. Among the reasons we don't is that dust buildup can cause spontaneous combustion, and inhaling the dust can lead to lung disease. Another reason is that our silos were made with cows in mind and goats eat a lot less grain. Our three-ton grain bin, which fits compactly inside our haymow, provides more than enough grain storage.

Rust has big eco-friendly plans for one silo, however. He wants to sink a stainless steel water tank into it and add solar panels on the silo cap, which would heat the water, as our propane boiler now does. Our other silo might house another venture (or folly) of Rust's: a coop for raising squab, or young pigeons (as opposed to the feral, copiously defecating kind that currently inhabit the huge space), for posh restaurants in New York City. Or else, he might use it to house birds of a different feather, creating an apartment tower for visiting Manhattanites.

When Marie Louise tackled the barn, the 1920s structure was in a significant state of disrepair. It hadn't been cleaned in years. Everywhere you turned, there was debris: scrap wood, rusted headlocks for keeping cows stationary, discarded machinery, crusted manure. Marie Louise got to work, cleaning out its interior and then hiring someone to whitewash the walls. Together, one late June afternoon, we moved several nineteenth-century oak beams, and I ended up in a hospital due to excruciating pain from a pinched nerve in my back. (Lifting heavy beams was quickly removed from my "to-do" list.) We fenced in the pasture in front of the barn, so our future goats could enjoy the outdoors but not the neighbors' gardens. There were, of course, some remaining challenges: The barn had neither electricity nor running water. For the first few months, we would fill the goats' water buckets by running a hose from the house to the barn.

Within two weeks, we brought Victoria, Magnolia, Iris, Lily, Zena, and Petunia to their new home. Immediately, I was on Marie Louise's case to make cheese. Fresh, creamy chèvre is what she'd made in France, so that was the natural choice. It is also the fastest and easiest cheese to produce from goat's milk, since it doesn't require any aging. She set to work, having special rennet express-mailed from France. Rennet is the enzyme that curdles milk, turning it into curds and whey—the first step in cheese making; she already came supplied with her own molds to shape the cheese. But then she pointed out a sticking point: We did not have a licensed, inspected cheese room.

"Use the kitchen," I said.

So she did, eventually spreading out into the dining room as well. I thought the result—a fresh chèvre—was excellent. I also loved the artistic way she liked to present it: on a lovely bed of leaves in a wicker basket.

The milk wasn't pasteurized, but as long as we didn't sell the chèvre, we were allowed to let friends and family taste it. (Since 1944, the U.S. Food and Drug Administration has required raw-milk cheese to be aged at least sixty days before being sold to customers.) I brought some back to New York City as a treat for chefs and friends, and Marie Louise took a batch home to New

Orleans one weekend, where unbeknownst to me, she hand-painted a cardboard sign and set up a stand at a farmers' market. (Now, that was risky!) It quickly sold out.

A promising beginning, but unfortunately, my debut cheese maker didn't last. Living in France for five years had refined Marie Louise's culinary sensibilities, so Vermont cuisine proved something of a disappointment. Plus, Vermont's cold weather was not to her taste. Then there was the fact that she was constantly getting hit on by our local bachelors. French farmers, she said, were more discreet, and Marie Louise wasn't even vaguely interested in any of them. I was pretty shocked that these men would not take no for an answer. They came back again and again with offers to take her canoeing, to the movies, hiking, hunting, and any other typical Vermont dating experience. One guy must have asked her twice a week. He just wouldn't go away.

The worst of the bunch was Randy, our handyman at the time. One day, Marie Louise said that he had walked into the kitchen, where she was making cheese, and asked, "Is it hot in here, or is it just me?" He then proceeded to remove his shirt and sidle up to her. She screamed at him, and he ran out the door. Randy didn't go only for younger women, as I later discovered. We were cleaning out the pens together on one occasion, and he gave me a strange grin, saying that his girlfriend was jealous of me because he "liked older women"—except that his language was considerably more graphic. I fired Randy in short order and after he returned to the farm, angry and shouting, I took out a "Notice of No Trespass" against him with the local constable. I often think about telling his girlfriend, but I've kept quiet.

By Thanksgiving 2003, Marie Louise was gone. But I promptly found someone to replace her. My second intern was Abby Rawlings, a recent agriculture graduate from Green Mountain College. The young woman requested a weekly salary of only $200. Rust and I were dumbfounded. I told her that we would pay $300, just as we had paid Marie Louise.

I WAS STILL CLUELESS ABOUT GOATS. DURING THAT EARLY phase, my time and energy were devoted overwhelmingly to my literary agency, and I had hoped at first that I could be the CEO of the farm, being present and making important decisions (Decision: Get goats; Decision: Make cheese) but delegating the follow-through responsibilities to talented subordinates. But as CEO, it hadn't occurred to me that the girl goats needed to get pregnant if they were going to produce milk to make cheese. Here it was late November—breeding season—and we were without the essential ingredient on which the entire operation turned: sperm.

I was quite in the dark about breeding. I didn't know how to tell whether a doe was in heat. (For the record, she's more vocal, twitches her tail a lot, and fights with her friends.) If you'd looked out the barn window that October—and every October since—you would see the gals rearing back and head-butting each other.

That's when they're not mounting friends and relatives. Yes, females will mount each other because they're so hot to trot. Rather than go into the breeding business in that first season, which would have required purchasing our first buck, Abby and I decided to rent a truck and schlep the girls back to the New Hampshire farm where we'd bought them.

They stayed there for several weeks, until they consummated their relationships with a couple of the farm's big boys and were ready to return home happy, pregnant, and considerably less horny.

THINGS WENT WELL FOR A WHILE: SEVEN MONTHS, TO BE precise. Abby was completely enthusiastic about the goats and the cheese making. But I made the mistake of letting her and her boyfriend move into the main house with Rust and me while we restored the smithy. I'd also done so with Marie Louise. This time, however, the close quarters probably hastened our split.

Abby wanted us to hire her boyfriend as well, claiming she was having to work too many hours, even though we were milking only nine goats at the time. A Deadhead, he'd sleep until noon, then meander out onto the porch in his pajamas and play his guitar all afternoon. I suffered his music silently until the couple sprang the news that they were leaving on a cross-country trip to follow one of their favorite bands. I expressed shock about a two-week vacation from a farm in June, but off they went, leaving me with all the farm duties.

But the straw that broke the proverbial camel's back occurred shortly after their return, when I discovered a "to-do" list I'd left Abby. (I'm big on "to-do" lists.) This particular one had been annotated by her boyfriend with obscene suggestions about what I could do with my chores. Abby's seven-month tenure on the farm ended seven hours after I discovered that list. It was one of the most awful things I'd ever had to do at that point—tell someone I wanted them off the farm when I knew that they had no job and nowhere to go. But the disrespect was only a minor motivation; more importantly, animals can't stop milking, and Abby was unreliable.

MY DAUGHTER, SAMANTHA, HAS A THEORY ABOUT MARIE Louise, Abby, and all the young women who have followed. She believes they are surrogate Sams and that I'm trying to fill the hole she would have occupied had she displayed more interest in the farm. I think, however, that although it could have been wonderful—practically and personally—to have my daughter as committed to the farm as I was, I certainly wasn't looking for surrogates. A farm needs hands, and unless the farmer has a trailer or other accommodation for workers, the farmhand lives in. It's not particularly convenient, but it's necessary.

Sam's disengagement with the farm became evident early on. That first summer in 2001, my hope was that she would be excited by the bucolic lifestyle. I'd even thought she might want to lend a hand, though I had the feeling that, if Sam had any designs on Consider Bardwell Farm, it would be as a yoga retreat. Whatever curiosity she might have had was destroyed when we met with Carol Delaney, a small ruminant expert in the Department of Animal Science at the University of Vermont. Sam and I visited UVM to get information on raising sheep and goats.

Inevitably, the subject of meat as a by-product of dairy farming came up. Goats have to give birth to produce milk and about half of those babies are boys. Although I have since tried to find homes for many of my newborn boys, that day we were reminded of the basic fact that they're normally slaughtered to be used as meat.

Sam, a vegetarian, went cold. It grew worse as Carol discussed animal husbandry and genetic chains. The instructor showed us charts and photographs of different udders and described how to breed for maximum udder size and milk production. The breeding process—and the superfluousness of all but those few breeding males to it—is something neither Sam nor, frankly, I had ever thought about before. She barely spoke on the long ride back to the farm, and from that day forth, she has had misgivings about the whole enterprise.

THE BOTTOM LINE FOR ME WHEN LOSING A WORKER, whether Marie Louise Ryan or Abby Rawlings, was this: I have had to pick up the pieces and learn to do her or his job, whether it was milking goats, stacking hay bales, or selling cheeses to restaurants and wholesalers. And so I gradually turned from hands-off management to fully engaged farmworker. Today, I could deliver a goat baby—and probably a human one, if I had to in the back of some New York City taxi.

One unanticipated benefit to all that sweat and labor was the twenty pounds I routinely lost every summer hoisting hay bales and showing powerful, strong-willed goats who's boss. After two months of heavy lifting and goat wrestling, by September, I'd be able to sport my size six skirts for Manhattan meetings—until the winter holidays, at least.

At first, I was particularly reluctant to tackle milking the goats. Marie Louise had wanted to teach me how as soon as we got them. But I declined. For some reason, the idea of messing with teats and udders, and the fear of doing something wrong and causing injury or infection, freaked me out. I myself had suffered from mastitis when I was a nursing mother, so I knew the pain of an infection firsthand.

The first time I was confronted with milking a goat on my own was Thanksgiving morning 2003. Abby Rawlings had just started working for me but hadn't yet quit her old job as a waitress. I had no choice but to take over—even so, I had a meltdown. The goats were misbehaving. They didn't want me milking them and resisted, especially Iris. Already insecure about my lack of milking technique, this spooked me even more. So I called a neighbor who'd milked cows by hand as a child—at that point we were still hand milking—and she came over and did it for me as I watched. Milking an animal is like riding a bike;

once you learn, you never forget. But learning to ride a bike at fifty-seven, my age when I started milking, is considerably harder than if you'd been taught when you were eight.

By the second year of goat herding, the drama was over. I could expertly and cheerfully take on the job whenever I needed to sub for one of the farmworkers who regularly handled this chore. These days, milking is among my favorite things to do on the farm. It reminds me of why we bought the property in the first place. Vermont is never as beautiful and peaceful as at dawn, when you step into your barn boots and walk to a distant pasture to retrieve the girls, then lead them back to the barn by flashlight to be milked.

DESPITE MY BUDDING SKILLS IN ANIMAL HUSBANDRY AND milking, I realized by early 2004 that what I really needed was a professional cheese maker. That's when my business connections paid off in a new way, and Peter Kindel entered the picture. Peter came recommended by Max McCalman. Max was one of America's leading cheese experts, and Peter had been his protégé at chef Terrance Brennan's top-rated restaurant Artisanal. From there, Peter had gone on to Murray's Cheese in Greenwich Village. Peter's wife, Caroline, had impressive food credentials of her own, having run Murray's wholesale operation and worked as a line cook at Craft, Tom Colicchio's heralded restaurant. The couple had even gone to Scotland's Isle of Mull to learn the art of cheese making themselves.

They had just had a baby in December 2003 and were ready to move on to their next adventure. They seemed a perfect fit. Peter would become our cheese maker and Caroline, with her marketing background and contacts, would sell the cheese. My only responsibility was to provide the financing. They were justifiably concerned about my ability to do that, so we struck a deal: I'd make them fifty percent partners and let them move into our Pond Cottage (not to be confused with the smithy, the cottage is directly across our pond as you look north out our kitchen window). I also agreed to let them take the first $50,000 in proceeds from cheese sales each year—the amount of money Peter calculated they'd need to live on.

I had nine milking goats in the summer of 2004: my original six, plus three others I'd bought from the same New Hampshire farm. I also purchased seven yearlings, who wouldn't be ready to give milk until May 2005. (They would breed in the fall, meaning they would have babies and produce milk six months later.) We had moved our cheese-making operations out of the kitchen to our newly built cheese room, which was certified by the State of Vermont in July. Even though we didn't have a proper aging cave, we had a customized walk-in cooler that would keep the cheeses at eighty-five percent humidity and 55°F.

Peter started making fresh cheese and selling it at farmers' markets in Manchester, Londonderry, and Dorset. We named our first cheese Mettowee, after our valley. He also started experimenting with aged cheeses. One result was Dorset, an aged raw-milk wash-rind cow's milk cheese. Washed rind describes cheeses that are ripened by washing the cheese with brine, wine, beer, brandy, or other liquid throughout the aging process.

Caroline made critical distribution connections for us: She was responsible for placing our cheese in some of the country's most famous restaurants, among them Daniel and Per Se. Because she had been selling to major restaurants from Murray's, they all trusted her judgment and palate.

When Caroline informed me that our Mettowee was on the menu at Per Se, owned by Thomas Keller, it felt surreal. Keller's chef, Jonathan Benno, had worked with Caroline at Craft and he was the one who put our cheese on the menu. On the one hand, I felt like an imposter—what gave our modest little farm, our fledgling cheese-making operation, and me in particular, a literary agent no less, any right to make cheese that graced the menu of one of America's most famous restaurants? But on the other hand, I was floating.

On one occasion I made a delivery to Per Se, which is located in the Time Warner Center and overlooks Central Park, and got to meet Jonathan. I'd never eaten there (and still haven't), but on that occasion he asked me if I'd like a copy of their tasting menu; there was our Mettowee! I felt like phoning Magnolia, Iris, Zena, and the rest of the "girls" back in Vermont to share my pride. I resisted the temptation but took the tasting menu, intending to have it framed. Unfortunately, in typically chaotic Consider Bardwell Farm fashion, I lost the menu before I got around to having it framed.

But Caroline's sales success turned out to be one of the few bright spots in her time on the farm. She was unhappy with Ver-

mont and worried about the farm's ability to sustain their livelihood. To make matters worse, she didn't have a driver's license.
Six months into the enterprise, Peter came to me and sadly gave
notice, saying that he was taking Caroline back to Colorado,
where her family could help with the task of child rearing—a
lonely endeavor on an isolated farm.

Because of the personnel turnover, I began to fear that Consider Bardwell Farm might be star-crossed. It was at such moments that Rust and I had to rely on blind faith, believing that,
despite any evidence to the contrary, this crazy enterprise was
meant to be.

After Peter Kindel came Ann Bridges. A local woman in her
forties, she had been working on the farm as Peter's assistant for
exactly two weeks when he and Caroline departed in October
2004. She had made fresh goat cheese only twice and had no idea
how to make aged cheeses. But she was stalwart—hardworking,
bright, and responsible. To help her out, I hired Peter Dixon,
whom Rust and I had met when we took a workshop he led on
starting a local cheese business. Brought on as a consultant, he
was to drop by every few weeks and share his know-how with
Ann.

Ann had raised goats, shown goats in competitions, started up
a 4-H Club in the town, and often hand-milked more than ten
goats twice daily. She knew a lot about milk and now wanted to
learn about cheese.

The problem was that Ann had never committed to work for
us full-time. Previously, she had chosen to stay home from work

for a few years, and now she feared her husband and son would miss her presence and home-cooked meals. What's more, she had health problems that put her out of commission for three and a half months at the beginning of 2006.

After Ann returned to the farm in April of that year, it wasn't long before she announced that she was taking another job. That was my lowest point with Consider Bardwell Farm. It wasn't just that Ann told me she was leaving; it was that she was leaving to work for a well-financed nonprofit foundation that aimed to start a local cheese-making operation and a goat farm as an educational facility for visitors.

The departures of Peter and Caroline and then Ann forced me to step into the process more than ever. I needed to prevent us from going under. But I did better than that; I helped expand the business.

I started taking cheese samples to restaurants myself. I would drive down to Manhattan and deliver cheese to my small but growing base of customers. These included Fred's at Barneys, the eatery inside the chic department store, Barneys. On shopping expeditions in previous years, I would arrive through the front door, walking past liveried doormen and double-parked limousines and town cars. Now I entered through the service entrance lugging coolers.

I enjoyed making a sale, but that had never been part of my business plan. Nonetheless, it was Rust who eventually pushed me to call Peter Dixon, who'd been our consultant for several years by that time. Originally, my intention was just to ask for hiring suggestions. I called and explained that I was looking for someone experienced and serious, and that I would pay whatever it took. As it happened, Peter was then trying to get himself out from under the debt of a previous failed cheese venture. He said, "What about me?"

So in January 2007, Peter started working for us full-time. Though his compensation is more than we've ever paid anyone, it's a bargain considering his cheese-making creativity, the hours he puts in, and his devotion to the business. Not only does he work like a dog, but he does so after driving from his home in Westminster West, a town on the opposite side of Vermont on the New Hampshire border near Brattleboro, about ninety minutes away. Along the way, he stops several times a week to pick up more than a dozen eighty-pound stainless steel canisters filled with cow's milk from Lisa Kaiman, owner of Jersey Girls. We purchase the entire production of this wonderful farm to make our cow's milk cheeses. Then on the way home in the evening, Peter delivers barrels of whey, the liquid remaining after milk has been curdled and strained, from that day's cheese production to a pig farm owned by one of Lisa's suppliers. Peter gets a side of pig each year in exchange for his generosity.

Having Peter on board, Rust feels vindicated in his theory that any time we lose somebody, we replace him or her with someone even better. I would agree to a point; I'd still hate to lose Peter Dixon.

EIGHT

the little farm that could

ON A HOT SUMMER DAY IN JULY 2008, I THOUGHT I'd get to do something I'd rarely done since acquiring our first goats: relax. On that particular day, my only responsibilities were to deliver cheese to several customers in Manchester and to check my email, which had been woefully neglected for several days. Because summer is usually a slower time for the publishing business, I was almost able to forget that I had another career.

The prospect for a relaxing day immediately evaporated when Debbie Tracy walked out. This was our *affineur*—the person who ran our cheese-aging cave. She quit because I refused to give her a raise (which would have been her second since starting only a few months earlier) in the form of "gas money" for her Chevrolet Silverado. Maybe my refusal makes me sound cheap, but Rust would have divorced me and Chris Gray would have quit had I given in to her demand.

Peter Dixon objected, too. As it was, I'd been paying Debbie nearly as much as Peter was making. It's true that Debbie was an incredibly hard worker and she ran the cave better than anyone before her. The cave is critical in the cheese-making process. It's in this climate-controlled room that cheese ages for weeks or months, developing mold as part of its natural aging process. That mold needs to be monitored and brushed off every couple of days. Debbie was truly dedicated: She would hold up a beautiful pink-hued wheel of polished Pawlet, beam with pride, and call it her baby.

She's talented at everything she takes on, in fact. But she doesn't have a diplomatic bone in her body. She groused constantly, about nearly everything and everyone—except Leslie, an eager pupil, whom she called "Pet." Leslie, in turn, adored her. She looked up to the older woman as something of a mother figure, praising how "up front" Debbie was—a trait her other coworkers didn't necessarily consider part of her charm.

If anybody bore the brunt of Debbie's departure (besides Leslie, who went into a funk for several weeks), it was Peter. Debbie had been his relief pitcher, doubling as cheese maker when she wasn't working her magic on the rinds in the cave. That had allowed Peter to leave on time and get home to his family.

With Debbie's abrupt departure, we were now understaffed. Typically in such situations, the cave operation is the first to suffer. You can't stop making cheese, since the milk will spoil if you don't turn it into cheese quickly. But there's a little more leeway with the cave. Nonetheless, Peter stepped up, putting his personal life on hold. He was now working six days a week—something he promised himself he would never do when he took this job, not after enduring similar experiences at previous farms where he'd worked.

Fortunately, Peter got help from Leslie, who rose to the occasion after she adjusted to Debbie's absence. The recent high school graduate not only pitched in in the cave, where she and Debbie had bonded, but also went to work as a cheese maker. Peter could now count on her to make a good batch of cheese without having to look over her shoulder.

Luckily, Margot Brooks also arrived within days of Debbie's departure. It was another case supporting Rust's belief in our farm's destiny. The young, fifth-generation farmer immediately began working in the cheese room alongside Leslie, and in September, her always-cheerful boyfriend, Alex, joined us as well.

Surprisingly quickly, things started looking up for us. We not only avoided imminent disaster, but we also soon had something to boast about.

I was returning from the Rutland farmers' market on July 26 and found Rust standing in the barnyard with a big grin on his face.

"Congratulations," he said.

Rust and I have an ongoing competition to see who can bring

home the most money from our respective farmers' markets in Londonderry and Rutland. I thought he was saying that no matter how badly I'd done, he'd done worse.

He said, "Congratulations. We won."

"We won what?"

He relished giving me the news: He'd just heard from a customer of ours, Catherine Bodziner, owner of Lucy's Whey, a cheese and specialty-foods shop in East Hampton, New York. She called from the American Cheese Society's annual competition in Chicago to tell him that one of our cheeses—the Dorset, a washed-rind cow's milk cheese—had just won a silver medal.

I was excited, but skeptical. I sent Rust into the house to look on the society's website to confirm that we'd won. Acting as if everything were normal, I unpacked the gear from the farmers' market, then started pacing in the barn. Part of me didn't believe it was true. The other part wondered, "Wait, second place? Why not first?"

Rust came out to announce that not only had the Dorset taken the silver in the washed-rind category, but our two other competition entries had also come away with silver medals: The Manchester, our tomme, a French Alpine semi-firm cheese, won in the aged goat cheese category, and Pawlet, a creamy cow's milk *toma*, garnered an American original–Italian style prize. It was a remarkable achievement to win medals in three categories, especially since this was the first year we'd entered any of our cheeses in competition.

I was especially thrilled about the Manchester. Both Pawlet and Dorset were cow's milk cheeses made from milk sourced from Lisa Kaiman's Jersey Girls farm, but the Manchester had been made in May from our freshly kidded herd. It was Consider Bardwell Farm cheese down to its very DNA.

It takes two months for Manchester to ripen, and the cheese had ripened to perfection. When we tested it before sending it off to Chicago, we realized it was excellent: soft, with butterscotch notes and an earthy bite. The industry recognition validated all our hard work. It made us feel as if we really did have something here. I started looking upon Peter Dixon as a star. Over the last two years, he had envisioned, planned, and crafted the winning cheeses. And he'd trained a cadre of cheese makers who could follow his lead.

As a matter of fact, Leslie turned out to be such a natural that her mother came by one day and confided that she wanted her to become a professional cheese maker. Indeed, Leslie could eventually take what she has learned with us and start her own goat cheese farm. At the tender age of eighteen, she had become an expert goatherd from working in the barn as well as a first-class cheese maker.

OUR SILVER MEDALS COULDN'T HAVE COME AT A BETTER moment—or, it turns out, at a scarier time. By early August, we were earning about $6,000 a week from farmers' markets, but spending $10,000 a week in salaries and other expenses. The main reason for this disparity was the tremendous amount of milk we were buying. Our milk bills were running $18,000 to $20,000 a month from Jersey Girls, Polymeadows Farm, and Noah's Arc Nubians, our suppliers. We agreed to increase our milk supply to make cheese for wholesale distributors as part of our growth plan. In order to have inventory to sell, we have to make the cheese three to four months in advance. I figured out that our milk bills would be running about $200,000 a year, and that didn't include the cost of raising our own goats for milk.

I knew we would have to increase production and expenses to grow, but the quantity of milk that came from our outside suppliers each month far exceeded how much had been estimated. Peter and his crew managed to keep up with the volume, but long days in the hot, steamy cheese room were stressing them out. Every week, the four cheese makers and one intern were turning out an amazing one hundred fifty Manchesters, fifty Dorsets, and a variety of other cheeses. But we were quickly running out of room in our caves.

By August, we'd filled up our second cave, which Rust had just built in May. Our situation was so serious that Peter had to rent a cave near his home and transfer one hundred wheels of Rupert, our most space-consuming cheese. (This aged raw cow's milk cheese weighs up to thirty pounds a wheel.)

I was so worried that I even considered shutting down the cheese-making operation for a while.

I called Peter into my office (the kitchen) and told him I couldn't go on buying milk. Peter and his team were overloaded, but he was also energized by the potential for critical and commercial success and suggested that I take out a line of credit. He reminded me that this is what manufacturing companies do when they increase production and what lines of credit are for. At certain times of the year, you're producing more than you're selling. At other times, you're selling more than you're producing; that is when you can pay back your loan and hopefully turn a profit.

That made sense, but I hated the idea of owing money; we had been debt-free so far. I had always financed the operation from the money we made selling cheese through my own savings and from Rust's sweat equity, which allowed us to avoid hundreds of thousands of dollars in plumbing, electric, and construction costs.

Besides, the problem wasn't a lack of demand for our cheese. To the contrary, we'd previously had to turn down orders from major companies such as Whole Foods, which wanted to carry our cheeses, but we just weren't making enough when the store chain wanted them. Now that we finally were, the cheese was piling up in our caves because we didn't have distribution deals in place.

The biggest problem, as Peter was quick to point out, was our lack of a sales network. We still hadn't engaged a wholesaler or a salesperson in addition to Chris Gray. Though we had a few restaurant and retail accounts in New York City, we were almost solely dependent on farmers' markets. But they came with restrictions. We could sell cheese made from our goat milk as well as milk from

Jersey Girls Dairy, with which we have a full production partner-
ship, but we couldn't sell cheese using Polymeadows' milk at New
York City farmers' markets, because they are producer-only markets, and Polymeadows' milk, delicious though it may be, isn't produced on our farm. Chris Gray had come up with a marketing plan
to set up business with wholesale distributors, but it wasn't set to
begin until September, a full month away. Chris had also mistak-
enly assumed we wouldn't have enough cheese to sell until the
early fall.

🐐

BY THIS POINT, CHRIS HAD BEEN WORKING AT CONSIDER
Bardwell Farm for three years. We first met in 2005, after I'd decided to sell our cheeses at New York City's farmers' markets and
needed a person to man our booth. I'd approached Sarah Post,
someone I knew from West Pawlet (who would learn to make
cheese for us under Peter's tutelage three years later). As much
as Sarah wanted to help, her social calendar was too full that
summer with weddings of friends and relatives. So she recommended Chris, a longtime friend. At the time, Chris seemed an
unlikely choice. In his midthirties, he had been working in the
music industry for more than a dozen years, most recently over-
seeing a couple of labels for Island Records, the company behind
Bob Marley and U2.

But he had been growing increasingly disenchanted with the
music business as the focus changed from developing artists to

obsessing over the bottom line. When we approached Chris about working with us, he embraced the idea.

Extroverted, with an impish grin—he always seems in on the joke—Chris had the personality for sales. But he also had some experience with cheese. During high school, he had trained as a cheesemonger while working at a cheese shop in his hometown of Worcester, Massachusetts. When living in Berkeley, California, one summer during college, he got a job with a small cheese maker and helped produce mozzarella and feta. The cheese business seemed to be his calling.

When looking at our cheese-making operation, Chris saw the seeds of what he had once admired about the music business: It presented an opportunity to turn people on to a product he believed in and make it relevant, desirable, even irresistible to the public.

"Cheese is an expression of what the farm is, in the same way that music is an expression of what a person's musical talent is," he said.

Chris was hired to handle one New York City farmers' market, but he expressed such wild enthusiasm for the farm that I invited him to help out in any way he could with marketing and sales. After he'd worked for us for two months, however, he got a call from EMI, one of the largest music labels, with an offer he couldn't help but consider seriously. They were offering an executive position with a mid-six-figure salary. The job would include flying all over the world with EMI's recording artists.

We were petrified of losing Chris. As so frequently happened throughout the course of our farm odyssey, he seemed to have arrived at just the right moment. We needed someone who understood marketing, could think strategically, and push us to the next level.

Chris's instinct was to stay with us, but the music job beckoned. He said, "It's hard to turn down the fat job, especially since there aren't these kind of jobs anymore."

The monthlong wait for Chris's decision tortured us. Rust, in his inimitable fashion, came up with a strategy for retaining Chris. "Just whisper one word in his wife's ear," Rust said. "Groupies!"

Fortunately, we didn't have to resort to guerilla tactics. Chris's wife, Laura Brown, worked in the music business, too; she was in sales with Warner Music Group, selling to places like Urban Outfitters and QVC. Laura was on our side. She knew how unhappy her husband had been over the past few years. She'd seen his growing dissatisfaction as the music business had dried up because of free file-sharing on the Internet. And Laura understood that the industry had become increasingly cutthroat as companies fought for a slice of an ever-shrinking pie.

In the end, Chris decided to throw in his lot with the hay-munching goats rather than the number-crunching record executives. That was January 2006. (Recently, we knew that he knew that he'd made the right choice when he and Laura bought a house in the village of West Pawlet, a mile down the road, planning one day—we hope in the distant future—to have a farm of their own.)

In exchange for choosing us over U2, we offered to make Chris a partner. He began organizing farmers' markets and establishing a strong New York regional customer base. He helped us plan the business in general, and also jumped into cheese making. We developed a routine in which Chris would come to the farm during the week and learn to make cheese while I was in the city, then return to the city on weekends to run the farmers' markets while I was at the farm. When Debbie quit in July 2008, Chris's ability to take up the slack as a cheese maker helped immeasurably. But it distracted him somewhat from his primary mission, which was to sell cheese.

After I had my heart-to-heart with Peter about turning off the milk spigot and he responded with a plea to drum up sales, I told Chris that his number one priority had to be fast-tracking some deals with cheese distributors by the end of August.

Chris jumped to it: He quickly made a deal with Provisions International, a wholesale distributor of specialty foods to western New York, western Massachusetts, and the rest of New England. He negotiated another deal with Cellars at Jasper Hill in Greensboro, Vermont, to distribute our Manchester and Dorset cheeses throughout the Midwest and western United States.

Mateo Kehler, who co-owns Cellars at Jasper Hill with his brother Andy, had been heralded in *The New Yorker* magazine the previous year as the superstar of American farmstead cheese making. In 1998, the two had taken over Jasper Hill Farm, a small place that had fallen on hard times in the Northeast Kingdom of Vermont. They tried and rejected several options for the farm—including making crafted beer and baked tofu—before finally settling on farmstead cheese. The Kehlers spent the next five years developing their knowledge and skills. The result was several prize-winning cheeses, among them Aspenhurst, a clothbound cheddar-style cheese. But their most important contribution may turn out to be their seven massive caves. Comprising twenty-two thousand square feet, these were built to age artisanal cheeses not just from their own farm, but from other small farms as well, including those that can't afford their own caves. In this and their cheese distribution work, the Kehlers are doing as much as anyone to save Vermont's farms and preserve the state's natural beauty.

Mateo already knew our cheese, and it didn't hurt that we had just won three silver medals. In late August, he came down to the farm to check out the operation and watch us make cheese.

After spending the day observing our various activities, Mateo was impressed enough to order fifty Manchesters and twenty Dorsets per week to start. He thought our relationship would be able to grow well beyond those numbers, but he wanted to be conservative at the beginning.

"Plan on me stopping in twice per month to select batches and get my hands in the vat," Mateo wrote in an email. "I feel like I need to be a party to the cheese and know the product and get to know your business if I am going to represent Consider Bardwell as well as it deserves."

He added: "The Manchester I brought home was off the hook." A hipster way of saying that it was great cheese.

In the course of a month, we went from a financial and personnel crisis to winning three silver medals and signing on with two of the most prestigious cheese distributors in the region and in the business.

The operation would no longer be hemorrhaging money. Soon, every Friday, a truck pulled up and took away our cheese. Our new distribution deals would pull in between $3,700 and $4,000 a week, which seemed enough to cover our milk bills of $15,000 a month.

The crisis was averted, but it made me wonder whether we were moving too fast. Our goal was to make fifty thousand pounds of cheese in 2008, and perhaps double that the next year. Was it realistic, given our facilities and manpower? We were a small farm, not a factory. Part of what made us special and helped win those medals were the complex flavors that can only come from using small-batch, artisanal methods of cheese making. As it turned out, I wouldn't have to continue my soul-searching in the months ahead. The souring economy and brake on consumer spending—especially with luxury items like handmade cheese—would save us from turning into Kraft.

husbandry

SEPTEMBER KICKED OFF WITH THE LABOR DAY WEEKEND
wedding of my friend and client, cookbook author Mark Bittman.
He had decided to grill goat for the Saturday night cookout that
preceded his Sunday wedding to Kelly Doe, an art director and
graphic designer at *The New York Times.*

So a week before the wedding, I took four male goats—two for
Mark and two for other customers—to the aptly named Over-the-
Hill Farm, a slaughterhouse in Benson, Vermont. They included
Peabody, who was Peony's son and the penultimate baby born in
April 2008.

Peabody was Laura's special love and for good reason; he was
gorgeous and sweet, big, healthy, and happy. My heart and
stomach were uneasy when I drove those twenty miles to the

slaughterhouse. I felt the same way I had in April, when I met up with Betsy Sinclair at Polymeadows Farm and sold her the season's first baby boys.

Our vet believes that one fundamental distinction between generational farmers and newcomers like myself is our attitudes toward killing animals. Traditional farmers think of their animals as beasts and producers. That doesn't mean they don't appreciate them and their idiosyncrasies. Those farmers may be as cognizant of the individual personalities of their goats, sheep, or cows as I am. They can point to a single cow in an eight hundred–animal herd, says Dr. Alderink, and tell you that this one will steal your hat, or that one only likes to be milked from the right side. On occasion, one of them will even become a pet.

I, on the other hand, tend to think of *all* my goats as pets; they are practically like furry humans who happen to produce copious amounts of milk. They're animals, of course, but they're definitely individuals with personalities who feel pain, happiness, satisfaction, sadness, and anxiety. They work hard for the farm, and they should be protected, kept healthy, and well cared for in return.

That said, Mark's wedding wouldn't be the first time I'd eaten one of our goats. I love the flavor; it tastes like lamb, but milder, and is far less fatty. Kid is commonly eaten in many ethnic communities and is hugely popular with trendy urban chefs.

Generational farmers are more efficient and unemotional, and I don't mean that as a criticism. No generational farmer would keep an animal like Lailani around. She would be culled, either by being given away or sold as a pet, or else "shipped," a euphemism for being sent to auction or slaughter, without a second thought. The money put into diagnosing Lailani's lameness and maintaining her throughout her pregnancy could conceivably have been spent buying two new milkers.

Generational farmers wouldn't even consider sending for the vet to treat a male kid, since they're worth virtually nothing. Betsy Sinclair paid me five dollars for each of the kids I dropped off in April. A single visit from the vet would far exceed their monetary value.

According to the vet, I am still in the process of transitioning from a city slicker (my term) to a country farmer mentality. My emotional attachment to the animals was apparent the Friday I met Mark Bittman in Killington, halfway between our farm and Barre, where he was having his wedding festivities.

I gave him his two goats—now skinned, quartered, and Cryovac-sealed. But I also brought the heads, packed separately, because I didn't want any part to go to waste. I've patted those heads, scratched their cheeks. It would have seemed sacrilegious to throw any part of them away. Chefs often boil them and use them for stew. But Mark didn't want the heads. He was afraid they would upset the young children staying at his future father-in-law's house. So I brought them back to the farm. I even knew which was Peabody's because of the large size of his head. I put them in the freezer in the barn until I could give them to a chef as a gift.

THINGS ONCE AGAIN WERE GOING SMOOTHLY ON THE FARM in September 2008. In fact, Rust and I were increasingly confident that we would be able to sneak away the next month to Piedmont, Italy, for another important wedding—of Steve Rich, one of Rust's friends from Cambridge. It would be the first time in two years that we could get away together.

We were selling lots of cheese at farmers' markets in New England, Westchester, and New York City, and even more through our new distributors. The staff had clicked. Sue Olsen was running the barn and caring for the animals with Alex's assistance, and Peter, Margot, and Leslie were making cheese six and sometimes seven days a week. Inspired by our silver medals and being at a point where we were covering our costs, the glorious goal of turning a profit seemed not only possible, but realistic.

Then, everything ground to a halt on Saturday, September 27, when the milking operation suffered the mechanical equivalent of a nervous breakdown. After all those years of devoted service (not always adequately recognized), it just couldn't go on any more.

I'd risen at 6 A.M., and when I didn't see Minny Buley's car pull into the barnyard by 6:15, I went out to the barn assuming I'd have to milk the goats myself. (Minny says she is afraid of the dark and refuses to leave her house, about forty-five minutes away, until there's light in the sky.)

Fortunately, Minny arrived a few minutes later and started the sanitizer, which runs a sterilizing cycle of the milking equipment.

We are required by law to do this within a half hour of using the milking system. After that, I was planning to take my car to Rutland for a 9 A.M. appointment to have new tires put on. (A few days earlier, I'd gotten a flat on the George Washington Bridge—not the most convenient place to change a tire.)

But before I could escape, Minny found me in the barn and told me that the vacuum pump that runs the milking equipment sounded funny. When I went to examine it, the motor was vibrating so violently I thought the belts were going to shake loose. I ran to the house, not looking forward to waking up Rust. But he was already at the kitchen table with his trusty cup of tea and computer, checking his favorite websites.

Rust knows motors and pumps. His father ran a machine shop, and the two of them would build devices together on weekends when Rust was a child. Those hours spent with his dad, who died when Rust was in his twenties, rank among his happiest memories.

Rust followed me back to the barn, took one look at the pump, turned it off, and pronounced it dead. For a couple of months now, my husband had been warning that we needed a new milking system. But we were hoping our current one would last through the season.

Rust told me to prep our backup system while he called Dave's Dairy Supplies in Hartford, New York. Dave Farrar, the owner, said he would deliver a vacuum pump in time for the machine to be ready to run for the evening milking.

In the meantime, there were forty-five goats needing to be

milked—immediately. Then we discovered that the backup system didn't work either. The last time we had used it was in the early spring, when we were milking the few goats who had their babies in advance of the others and it didn't make sense to start up the main milking system for such a small number. But the equipment hadn't been washed and drained properly before being packed away, and some sort of black gunk or mildew had formed. Disgusting, but that could be fixed. Worse was that there was no suction to the inflations, the cups that attach to the goat udders.

By now it was 8:30 or 9 A.M. and the goats were screaming. Rust had canceled my tire appointment before heading out to sell cheese at the Londonderry farmers' market, but now Minny and I were faced with the prospect of hand-milking forty-five unhappy goats. Minny suggested I call Leslie and Amber. Leslie was unavailable, but Amber said she'd be right over. I also roused Margot and Alex, which I hated to do because it was their day off. The young couple was out of bed and over to the barn in a flash. But after one of the goats knocked over a pail that Alex was using, he remembered a pasture in urgent need of fencing and said good-bye. Luckily, Margot was a champion hand-milker—having done it since she was about nine years old—and she more than picked up the slack. By 11:30, having hand-milked the girls into buckets four at a time, we were done.

Unfortunately, we had to throw away all the milk because of one vital detail: There had been no time to sanitize the buckets. Besides, with hand-milking it's virtually impossible to keep all the hair and dirt from the goats' udders from falling into the milk. On top of that, probably half the girls kicked over their buckets in indignation, not being used to hand-milking.

Dave Farrar dropped off the new pump and Rust, back from the farmers' market, had it installed and ready to go by 5 P.M. When we tried to start it up, however, the pressure gauge refused to move past zero. It seemed the motor that powered the pump was on the blink.

"Fuck it!" said Rust, his British accent making four-letter words sound slightly genteel. He immediately realized that the problem all along had been with the motor, not the pump. "Where the fuck are we going to get a motor before we have to leave for Italy?"

We had plans to depart that Wednesday, four days later.

Dave Farrar said he had an old motor. But that night Rust went online and found a new one for sale somewhere near the Canadian border, a drive of several hours. The next day, Rust and his assistant, Geoff Miles, left for Canada, abandoning their plan to install a new wood-burning fireplace and stove in our dining room.

This is why holes in the farm's walls and ceilings never seem to get filled. It's why shiny new appliances sit in our barn, their boxes unopened, for years. Rust spends so much time addressing emergencies that any noncrisis project gets shunted aside for another day. (That, and the hours he devotes to reading about politics and railing at the powers that be. Then again, it's his weekend, too.)

In the meantime, I went out and bought a brand-new pulsator for our backup system, so Amber and I used it on Saturday evening, then again on Sunday morning and evening. We tossed all that milk, too.

Rust and Geoff returned from Canada on Sunday night, September 28, with our new milking machine motor. They walked through the milk-house door, where I was just finishing cleaning the backup milking system, and Rust demanded, "What's for dinner?"

By that point, I'd been working nonstop since 5 A.M. "I've been on my feet for sixteen fucking hours," I snapped (without the genteel lilt). "All you've done is sit in a car. Make your own dinner!"

Given the circumstances and our exhaustion, we both let it go.

Rust worked on the motor all day Monday and had it installed for the evening milking. By Tuesday we were on our way down to New York City, and on Wednesday we departed for Italy. Our spat and trouble behind us, we spent the next eight blissful days at the Cenobio dei Dogi, a lovely hotel overlooking the Mediterranean in Camogli, a fishing village on the Italian Riviera near Genoa. The most delightful thing about it was that I didn't receive any alarming news from the farm, only a couple of emails to let us know that everything was running smoothly—and that the U.S. economy was nearing collapse.

LITTLE COULD I HAVE GUESSED WHEN WE FIRST MET IN 1981 that Rust's mastery of pumps and motors would play a vital role in our relationship. It was at a birthday party for people born in January. I was; he wasn't. He had been brought to the party by Gavin Hogben, a January baby and friend from Cambridge who had also moved to America. To this day, Gavin is Rust's business partner and best friend.

I was attracted to Rust from the moment I met him. I had a thing for British guys ever since I'd done my junior year abroad at Oxford. His eccentric appearance also appealed to me. He was wearing a Baltic sea captain's hat, an old navy overcoat that was belted in the back, and a pair of round, wire-rimmed, John Lennon glasses that were available for free from the British National Health.

Rust was tall with high ruddy cheekbones. It was shocking when he took off his cap and had no hair underneath. Making light of having lost his hair at a young age, he said, "It's soft as a baby's hiney." He's witty under normal circumstances, and even wittier when he has had something to drink. He'd had a lot to drink that night and was extremely witty. We talked from 7 P.M. through dinner at midnight until two the next morning. That was long enough for me to know that I wanted to be with him forever. I even called friends the next day and said, "I met the man I'm going to marry."

I had been married once before, when I was in my early twenties. Samantha, born in 1971, was my daughter from that first marriage. Although burned by that experience and unattached from the time of my divorce in 1977 at age twenty-seven until four years later when I met Rust, that night I just knew he was it.

Unfortunately, Rust wasn't as immediately convinced as I was that he'd met his life partner. He took my number, but when he didn't call (he was still recovering from a recent breakup), I phoned him a couple of weeks later.

Our first date was on Valentine's Day. We went to an exhibit of Korean ceramics at the Metropolitan Museum, then to a movie, and then to dinner at La Bonne Soupe, an unpretentious restaurant in the West Fifties, which still exists around the corner from where we live today. We continued dating, but we didn't get serious until that summer, when we rented a house on Shelter Island with fourteen other people, many of whom remain our friends to this day. We moved in together in the fall.

Rust and I didn't get married, though, until December 30, 1984, in Cambridge, where Rust, who still had his college apartment, was spending the month. It wasn't an elaborate ceremony, to say the least; perhaps that's because I'd given him an ultimatum a couple of months earlier: The relationship was over unless he agreed to get married by the end of the year. "Why would we get married?" he demanded. "We're getting along so well." I said that if we don't get married, we're going to get along less well. So he agreed, on our trans-Atlantic phone call, on the condition that I keep the wedding secret.

I was hurt, but motivated to agree. My gut instinct and

almost four years of living with him told me we belonged together.

Besides, I didn't keep my word. I *couldn't* keep my word. I was too excited. As soon as I got off the phone with him, I screamed to my colleagues at The Miller Press, my little book-packaging company and literary agency, "I'm getting married!"

Our witnesses were Pam and Peter Czerniewski, British friends who had moved back to England from New York. Our reception—if it could be called that—was held at the Pickerel, a Cambridge pub, and was limited to the Czerniewskis and Samantha, who was thirteen at the time and had flown over with me.

The marriage didn't get off to a smooth start. Rust and Sam returned to the U.S. a couple of days after New Year's while I stayed in London to do book business. But almost as soon as Rust got off the plane, he ran into Dave Gibbons, one of my colleagues at The Miller Press, who said, "Congratulations!"

Rust was so angry that I'd broken my word about keeping mum that he wouldn't talk to me for weeks. It eventually required getting Dave Cook, an old friend from Cambridge, to intercede on my behalf.

Rust maintained the secret on his end—quite successfully. He didn't even tell his own family, who lived in England. His two older sisters came to visit us a couple of months after our wedding, and they still didn't know. I told him that he was being ridiculous and had to break the news.

"There's something I have to tell you," he shouted to them from the kitchen. Sitting with me at the dining room table, they grabbed my hand; they knew instantly what he was going to say. "We got married."

His sisters were happy for us, but immediately thought he was ashamed of them; they couldn't imagine why else he had gotten married in England and never let them know nor invited them. Meanwhile, I thought he was ashamed of me. But I think the explanation is simpler. Rust, like a lot of men, had to be dragged to the altar. He had enjoyed being a bachelor, didn't want children, and wanted to keep his options open. He even refused to exchange rings until 2005, when I told him all I wanted for Christmas was my own wedding ring.

Despite his foibles, I love and admire my husband. He has come a long way from Slough, the working-class town twenty miles west of London, where he was born in 1946. He was the youngest of four children, by a lot—his closest sibling was seventeen years older. Rust's father, who built tanks during World War II and kept running the machine shop that built those tanks after the war, was born in 1900.

Rust scored well on high school entrance exams and was sent to an experimental high school, where he was exposed to everything from theater to engineering. That's where he decided to become an architect. Rust tried to get a job with an architectural firm once out of high school. But he couldn't afford to take an unpaid internship—the only kind he was offered—so he found work with an air-conditioning company. Finally, at twenty-three, he found a position with a London architectural firm, Roy Hope Associates. He had never really considered applying to architecture school—at the time, it was still very much an upper-class, tweed suit, Victorian profession—until a colleague at the firm who was then doing his "practical year" apprenticeship for Cambridge suggested that Rust apply to the venerable university.

"You're smarter than half the guys up there," he told Rust.

It took some courage to apply. Despite the seismic changes taking place in British society in the early 1970s, Cambridge remained a bastion of elitism and privilege. Most of the students still came from posh boarding schools, or "public schools" as they're called in Great Britain, such as Eton. Rust feared he stood little chance of gaining admission through formal channels, even though he'd gotten five "A Levels," the highest score on Britain's high school graduation exams. So instead, he simply showed up early one morning at the home of Sir Leslie Martin, one of England's most esteemed architects and head of Cambridge's architecture school at the time.

"I knocked on the back door," Rust remembers. "He wasn't expecting me. He opened the door in his dressing gown, bleary eyed, and said, 'Yes?' I announced, 'I want to be an architect.' He said, 'Come on in.' "

Rust had his portfolio with him, or what passed for a portfolio: charcoal sketches, architectural models, even some pottery he had made. Sir Leslie also seemed impressed by Rust's life experience. Most of the school's candidates were only seventeen or eighteen—fresh out of high school. Rust, five years older, had already seen a bit of the world and held down a steady job.

After talking to Rust for about half an hour, Sir Leslie was sufficiently impressed that he wrote a name down on a piece of paper, the director of studies at Cambridge, and said, "Go see this guy."

He was accepted, and it turned out to be quite an adjustment. In that first year, Rust was in the bottom third of his class, and Sir Leslie probably worried he'd made a mistake in advocating for him. Rust lacked the technique of his fellow students and, just as significantly, people skills. That's critical in architecture, where personal presentation is almost as important as talent in gaining commissions. Some of Rust's peers were among the most brilliant people he'd ever met. Some weren't. Nonetheless, socializing was second nature to most of them. "They could stand up for three hours and speak about nothing," Rust recalls.

Rust kept at it. British university students do three years at their college, then a "practical" or work year. After that, they return to university for two more years and a master's degree. Rust showed enough progress on all fronts by his practical year that Peter Bicknell, the architecture faculty's director of studies and a famed architect in his own right, hired him to work at his Cambridge firm. By 1978, the year Rust graduated, he received a "first," or highest honors, a distinction given to only four of that year's forty architecture graduates. He also received an architecture prize and was made a Scholar of Downing, the name of his college at the university.

By outward appearances, Rust appears laid-back, but in fact he can be intense and extremely competitive—however, he backs that up with talent. He has managed quite well through word-of-mouth recommendations from clients. His commissions have ranged from hedge-fund manager mansions in the Hamptons to Robert Redford's Fifth Avenue apartment.

SO I CAN'T SAY THAT RUST'S TALENTS HAVE REACHED THEIR apogee or met their match at Consider Bardwell Farm. But the challenges here have kept him occupied—and sometimes happy—on weekends, between resurrecting the barn, building our caves, sourcing and installing much of the cheese-making machinery, and keeping it running smoothly—and doing so as cheaply and environmentally consciously as possible.

"I like to have these projects running the whole time," Rust says. "That's what I've done since I was a kid with my dad. I was always happiest when we were out in the garden and he said, 'Let's build a fish pond or a garden chair.' "

Both Rust and I have strong personalities, so our marriage has gone through some rough patches. His months-long refusal to publicly admit we were married was a red flag, but it's not my nature to back down from a challenge when I believe in something—neither from a bullheaded boyfriend nor from my choice of city mouse–country mouse lifestyle.

To Rust's credit, he worked with me through my family crises, even after one of our biggest blowups when I first told him I wanted to sell Spring Gardens, the house on Shelter Island, and leave the island completely. Rust loved everything about the place—the porch life and socializing with our neighbors, lying in the hammock and watching birds fly in and out of the eaves, his flourishing rose garden—but he joined me for this farm adventure.

NOW, I CAN SAFELY SAY THAT CONSIDER BARDWELL FARM has filled the void left by the loss of our island home. The farm is actually so all-consuming that it's like the child we never had together. In fact, the challenges we face here dwarf anything we confronted at our gingerbread Victorian on Shelter Island; working the farm feels less like raising a child and more like caring for octuplets.

Part of what I think makes the farm intellectually compelling for Rust is that it's an organic process; he's learning as he goes along. Not about architecture; he got that down a long time ago. Rather, he's learning about animal husbandry, cheese making, cheese aging—and crafting architectural solutions to the special problems that goats and cheese present.

It's almost a synthesis of what he learned at Cambridge and what he picked up at his father's side. As a small child, Rust wondered whether there was some way to link the two fish ponds they'd dug in their backyard in Slough, so the fish could travel between them. His father nodded, and they dug a tunnel connecting the two.

In fact, because everything has been such an organic, trial-and-error, by-the-seat-of-your-pants process, Rust knows much more now than when we started with the goats six years ago. His temptation at this stage is to rebuild the cheese-making operation from the ground up, employing gravity-based systems to enhance the efficiency of our operation and reduce energy consumption.

He would like to rebuild the entire milking operation on a downward slope, with the milking parlor at the highest point, the storage tank in the middle, and the cheese room below. The milk could flow from one end to the other without pumps or motors, using a fraction of the energy that the system does now.

Rust claims he'd be able to pull it off without losing a single day of cheese making. He'd simply build the new operation in a lean-to alongside the old one, taking the old equipment off-line only when the new equipment was ready to go.

I don't know if this will ever happen, but imagining it keeps him happy. If it does materialize, I have no doubt that Rust will find a way to get the government to help defray the cost. As a matter of fact, the farm has triggered a talent I didn't know Rust had: landing government grants. That can be as important to the survival of today's family farm as producing children to provide free labor was in the past.

OUR RELATIONSHIP WITH THE NONPROFIT ORGANIZATION Efficiency Vermont started a few years back when Rust was leafing through his new favorite publication, the USDA's *Agreview*.

The bimonthly covers such topics as farm-labor wages and how to increase egg production. Rust came across a small ad that said, "How would you like to replace your light fixtures free of charge?"

Being a cheapskate, he certainly did; our barn was filled with dusty old eight-foot fluorescents.

Rust called the number on the ad, though skeptical it might be an identity-theft scam. But there was no catch. Rust bought two energy-saving light fixtures, and Efficiency Vermont sent him a check. He went out and bought ten more fixtures, and they sent him a bigger check. Efficiency Vermont's thinking, apparently, is that they would prefer to buy new lightbulbs for everyone who asks rather than see Vermont come to need a new billion-dollar power plant.

Eventually, Rust replaced the barn's entire lighting system with energy-efficient lamps. He then began investigating what else he could get for free, and he had energy-saving ideas of his own. His first was to cool our cheese caves using a radiant cooling system that would run through the pipes in the cave walls. It's the same concept as radiant heating, except instead of pumping hot water through pipes to heat a room, you pump cold water to cool it. The folks at Efficiency Vermont seemed charmed by the idea, or perhaps by the fact that Rust had actually read their literature. When Rust asked whether there might be a grant available for such a project, they said, "Sure."

Rust's system would require a chiller—essentially an air conditioner that runs on water. He tracked down some chillers online, but they were all industrial sized. Even the smallest were triple the size we needed. But he eventually located a company in the Midwest that had created a small experimental unit for a Chicago nightclub to chill their vodka behind the bar.

It sounded ideal. Rust negotiated, and they eventually agreed to build a unit to his specifications for $5,000. Efficiency Vermont agreed to pay for more than a third of the cost.

Rust also discovered the USDA's Conservation Reserve Program. Through the CRP, the government was willing to subsidize the cost of fencing that would prevent our farm animals from wandering into the brook and polluting the water supply. At that time—2005—we had just gotten enough animals to make us think we needed a bigger pasture, and the pasture we had in mind behind the farm was surrounded on two sides by water, making it an ideal candidate for protective fencing.

The only condition was that we had to leave a thirty-five-foot strip of land, known as a filter strip, between the fence and the water. But the government was even willing to pay us a small annual stipend to keep that land vacant. In the end, between the CRP, the U.S. Fish and Wildlife Service, and other agencies, the government covered one hundred percent of the $6,000 fencing.

The way the government decides how it's going to allocate grant money is based on a point system. Farmers accumulate points by committing to and completing government projects on time and on budget. We started off with zero points. Eight years later, we now have so many points that Efficiency Vermont and the USDA call us with ideas. We were dumbfounded when Sally Eugair, a soil conservation technician with the USDA, told us that we've had more projects with them than any of the other nine hundred farms in the state.

Our most ambitious project began in 2007 with a casual conversation. A farmer who leased one of our fields to grow corn was trying to accumulate points to build a multimillion-dollar methane generator on his property; this would provide energy by burning cow manure. He mentioned that he could get points by protecting the riverbank along the field he leased from us.

The riverbank didn't deserve protection, as Rust later pointed out to both the farmer and the USDA. The river's contours were totally artificial. What had once been a meandering stream had been straightened over the years by berms constructed to redirect its flow, which prevented flooding in the adjacent cornfields.

But the whole point of the government program was to wean farmers of their dependence on corn and reduce its detrimental side effects. These included the depletion of soil and the pollution of the water supply with herbicides used to produce perfect ears.

So it turned out that we could get a large grant to return the river to its original contours. The government would cover the cost of removing the berms, which would not only allow the river to follow its age-old course, but also return the surrounding cornfields to excellent pasture. Part of that process was letting the river flood once again—a practice that dates back to medieval times, as one of Rust's Cambridge friends pointed out. This kind of pasture is called a "summer meadow." After flooding in the spring, the water retreats in the summer but leaves behind all the nutrients it deposited there, making it ideal pasture for goats.

We went to the USDA's offices in Rutland and were sitting around the conference table discussing the project when Rust, in his inimitable direct fashion, asked how much money might be available. He said he'd heard there might be an incentive payment. "Yes, $30,000," one of the government officials replied. I almost fell out of my chair.

Not only that, but the USDA would pay $2,800 a year to keep a strip of land adjacent to the river clear, as they had with our fencing grant. On top of that, they would give us another $7,000 if we agreed to convert the field to organic pasture, which we planned to do anyway. They'd also pay us to prepare the ground, seed it, and use organic fertilizer. In the end, that project won us $54,000 in grant money. It felt like a life preserver, coming at a time of year—the winter months—when cash flow was always a problem. We could use the money paid up front as we needed it, as long as we completed the project according to our agreement. The farmer who tipped us off about the whole thing also came away satisfied.

These days, representatives from the USDA and Efficiency Vermont routinely drop by with papers to sign or new programs to talk about. They always come on Monday mornings, when they know both Rust, a font of good ideas, and I, receptive to any plan that makes us money, will be around with pens in hand.

the way of the
cheese master

ONE DAY IN OCTOBER 2008, A TEAM FROM OUR DISTRIB-
utor Provisions International came to watch the cheese-making
process—and Peter Dixon's casual mastery of it. We were making
Rupert, our Swiss Alpine–style hard cow's milk cheese.

"Great cheese starts with great milk," explained Peter, who
modestly credits the quality of our milk rather than his own
knowledge and craftsmanship for the accolades our cheeses have
garnered.

Here in a nutshell is how we make cheese: We start with fresh
milk, heat it, add bacteria cultures to convert the milk sugar to lactic acid, then add rennet (an enzyme) to coagulate the milk. Together the cultures and rennet turn the milk into a gel-like

substance; sharp blades then cut the gel into curds, expelling the whey (the watery liquid that milk sheds after it has been curdled). The curds are put into molds and pressed to remove remaining whey. The cheese is then brined to prevent contamination and add flavor (unless it's a fresh cheese, in which case it's just salted) and then aged in caves.

Peter began his routine: He started by pouring 1,290 pounds of creamy Jersey cow milk into our 150-gallon cheese vat (8.6 pounds of milk equals one gallon). The cow's milk Peter gets is fresh from the farm: Every morning on the way to work, he picks it up in ten-gallon stainless steel milk cans from our partner Jersey Girls Dairy in Chester, Vermont, and crosses the Green Mountains to bring it to our farm.

This may seem like a huge amount of milk, but here's what it means in terms of the yield for a large cheese like Rupert:

The basic rule of thumb for cheese is that ten pounds of milk will make approximately one pound of cheese. Rupert, literally our biggest cheese, weighs in at thirty pounds per wheel. It requires three hundred pounds of milk for every wheel produced, which means we ultimately get roughly four wheels of cheese per vat. It's a lot of work, but it's worth it.

THE CHEESE ROOM WHERE THE MAGIC HAPPENS ISN'T large—about 15 x 15 feet—but it's bright, with white walls, a cement floor, and a stainless steel cheese vat in the center of the room. There's a sink to wash cheese-making equipment and tables to press and drain the cheese.

There are windows, of course. One set faces north and offers a view across the barnyard to the smithy and our red brick farmhouse beyond that. The other faces west, opening onto the pasture behind the barn where the goats are grazing and to the hills beyond.

In many respects, the cheese-making process is strenuous and stressful. You've got to be on top of many things at all times, keeping close tabs on the milk's temperature and coagulation rate as it turns to curd. The room can get steamy on hot summer days and quite chilly during Vermont's dramatically cold winters, even though it's air-conditioned in summer and heated in winter.

But there's also something absorbing and lovely about the process: the brightness of the room, the pungent smell of the curdling milk, the gentle whirring of the blades in the cheese vat. Its all-consuming nature seems to make the rest of the world recede into irrelevance.

It takes more than heat and motion to make great cheese. The chemical processes that turn humble milk into artisanal cheese costing $24 per pound don't start until the temperature of the milk reaches 70°F. At this point, Peter pours in the freeze-dried starter cultures and the magic begins.

Cultures are the bacteria we add to milk to ferment it—that is, to turn the sugar in the milk to lactic acid, which gives it the sour taste we associate with cheese and yogurt. Certain cheeses, such as Rupert, require cultures that work best at high temperatures, typically above 90°F. These are known as "thermophilic" cultures, and we use four different varieties.

We buy our cultures from Glengarry Cheesemaking and Dairy Supply in Canada, which in turn imports them from a company called Danisco in France. Once you join the cheese community, there are certain names you hear again and again, and Margaret Morris, owner of Glengarry, is one of them. She is a mother figure of sorts to North American cheese makers. You can call Margaret with any cheese-making question and be assured that she'll listen and help.

Some of the art and science of cheese making involves knowing which cultures to use and at what temperatures. When producing cheese in small batches—that is, when approaching it as a craft rather than an industrial enterprise—the art comes in getting the quantities and temperatures right relative to the composition of the milk, which can be a moving target. Milk composition, which is really the protein, fat, mineral, and (good) bacteria content, varies from month to month, farm to farm, sometimes even animal to animal. For example, when Peter made some Manchester cheese a few days before the cheese demonstration, he could immediately tell the difference between our milk and the fattier milk from Polymeadows Farm, which was reserved for the Manchester tommes we made especially for Jasper Hill's distribution in the West. He knew the difference just by looking: With its higher fat and protein content, the Polymeadows milk formed into a firmer curd than ours.

There are other ways of knowing. One is by lab analysis. Once a month, we send a milk sample to the central labs of Agri-Mark, a dairy co-op in West Springfield, Massachusetts. It takes about a week to get back their analysis of our milk's composition.

Another method is by knowing what the goats are eating. Ours get their nutrition primarily from fresh, grazed grass. That means the fat and protein content of their milk will be low. In contrast, the nine Nubian goats at Noah's Arc, a small milk supplier of ours, feed exclusively on hay, which gives their milk the highest fat and protein content. Polymeadows is somewhere in the middle, since its goats dine on a combination of hay and fresh grass.

Breed is also a factor. The milk produced by our Oberhaslis is not particularly high in fat and protein, no matter what they eat. Polymeadows raises a variety of breeds, so the combination of its milk results in a product that is higher in fat and protein than ours. And the Nubian breed, the only breed Noah's Arc Nubians raises, is known for the extremely high fat and protein content of its milk.

A good cheese maker knows these variables intimately. When making Manchester, to get the same result with our milk as with Polymeadows', Peter had to adjust the temperature (95°F for ours versus 92.5°F for theirs). If Peter had cooked Polymeadows' milk at 95°F, the resulting cheese would have been too firm because of the milk's higher fat and protein content.

ABOUT THIRTY MINUTES AFTER ADDING THE CULTURES, Peter adds the rennet. Rennet is an enzyme that breaks down the milk proteins, which then coagulate—that is, reconnect—in more solid form. Together the cultures and rennet turn milk into curds. After the addition of rennet, the conversion process will continue over the next twenty-four hours—both inside the milk vat and on the cheese room's pressing tables once we remove the cheese from the vat—until Peter lowers the cheese into the brine.

The visible sign that the process is working is when you see the curds coagulating and expelling watery whey. We like to keep the milk agitating at very low speed—stirrers in the milk vat do that—until shortly after we add the rennet. We let the rennet mix into the milk for three minutes, then turn off the agitation and check for flocculation, a stage in the coagulation process when the liquid begins to congeal; that takes about fifteen minutes. Movement will resume only when we replace the stirrers with blades and start to cut the cheese. Any kind of movement while the rennet is still working its magic would disrupt the curd formation and create curd particles of different sizes. A nonhomogeneous curd formation makes the texture of the cheese defective.

For a long time we used rennet in liquid form, which was derived from the stomach lining of nursing calves. This lining slows down the digestion process, so that infants—be they cow, goat, or human—are able to extract the maximum amount of protein from the milk.

I had been surprised when I first learned about the source of rennet; I envisioned little calves being sacrificed just to make cheese. That's not the case, of course. Rennet is one of the by-products of veal production. Nowadays it goes into all kinds of things beyond cheese. Most packaged puddings in the supermarket use rennet, for instance. Nonetheless, rennet's origin was yet another unpleasant fact I would have to acknowledge and come to terms with in my role as a food producer.

A simple, if unappetizing, way of understanding rennet's role in the cheese process is this: Imagine a human baby burping. The milk that comes back up doesn't look like it did going down; it has been transformed into curds. The digestive enzymes in the baby's stomach lining have worked on the milk. The same thing occurs in calves, and the use of calves' rennet has long been a part of the cheese-making process.

The origins of cheese are unknown, but they might date as far back as 8,000 B.C., when sheep were first domesticated. Predating recorded history, we must rely on legend to imagine cheese's beginnings, and the most common story is this: Some ancient traveler put milk into a portable container made from a young ruminant's tummy. After trudging in the heat for several hours, the nomad pulled over for a refreshing drink and discovered, undoubtedly to his dismay, that the combined forces of heat, motion, and rennet had turned his milk into curds and whey.

Despite the history and tradition behind animal rennet, Consider Bardwell Farm stopped using it in January 2008. That was my daughter Samantha's doing. She told Peter that she wished she could eat our cheese but, as a vegetarian, didn't see how she could as long as we used animal rennet.

Peter, who had used animal rennet throughout his first year here in 2007, agreed to perform an experiment: He made a batch of each cheese—Dorset, Pawlet, Rupert, and all the rest—using two different rennets: traditional animal rennet and vegetable rennet. The latter is a microbial coagulant derived from a fungus called *Mucor miehei*. If he couldn't tell the difference between the two batches, he agreed to switch.

There is actually some debate about whether vegetable rennet works as well as the animal variety. English cheese makers are adamant about using only animal rennet when making traditional clothbound cheddar, according to Peter. They believe vegetable rennet lends the cheese a bitter taste.

One of the original vegetable rennets, still in use by some cheese makers in Spain, was made from the carduna plant, also known as the cardoon or artichoke thistle. Peter also knows a Maine cheese maker who brought some seeds back from Europe, grew a field of it, and made rennet from the flowers.

In any case, even with all of Peter's experience, he couldn't tell the difference between his test batches—with any of our cheeses. True to his word, he agreed to use vegetable rennet from then on.

Of course, there's a fundamental flaw in Sam's logic, though I'd never dare point it out to my dear daughter. It's true that using vegetable rennet avoids harming animals. But the milk that goes into making our cheeses still comes from the bodies of goats and cows. Neither animal lactates spontaneously. They must have babies, and fifty percent of those babies are boys, destined for slaughter.

But if using vegetable rennet gives Samantha or any other vegetarian cheese lover greater peace of mind, I'm all for it.

🐐

ONCE THE RENNET IS INTRODUCED, THE NEXT PHASE OF the cheese-making process is flocculation. This part of the coagulation process—when the milk starts to turn into a gel—takes between twelve and eighteen minutes. It's important to track that time precisely from cheese to cheese, because it tells the savvy cheese maker when to cut the curd—that is, to separate the curds (solids) from the whey (liquids). There are specific formulas based on the type of cheese you're making. Knowing them allows the cheese maker to adapt to changes in the density of the milk.

For example, with a soft cheese such as Dorset, if it takes fifteen minutes for flocculation to occur, you know you have to wait four times that (sixty minutes) before it's ready to cut. With a harder cheese such as Rupert, we cut sooner; if it takes fifteen minutes for flocculation, we'll wait only an additional ten minutes before cutting.

It's standard practice to perform a simple test to determine whether flocculation has occurred: You take a small plastic dish, set it atop the now-gelatinous substance, and try to spin it. When the dish no longer spins, that means the milk has gelled and you can predict when you're ready to start cutting it into curds.

The transition from milk to gel happens in just a few seconds;

the actual point of flocculation is that quick! (If you like food science, this is a great moment to watch closely.)

Cutting begins when you crank up the speed of the blades in the cheese vat. The combination of cutting for five to ten minutes and heating, which usually takes about an hour, causes the curds to contract and squeezes out the whey. The vat itself is ringed by a thermal metal jacket containing a spray-ring pipe with tiny holes that spray hot water inside the metal sheath, thereby heating the curds. The harder the cheese you're making, the smaller the curds should be, because smaller curds retain less water. Conversely, larger curds mean more water and softer cheese.

Dorset is our softest cheese. It's pliant, elastic, and, when left at room temperature for a few hours, it bulges out at the cut. It is buttery, but not runny. To achieve this consistency, the curds have to be as large as possible. In fact, there's no way we can get our blades to cut them as large as needed—into one-inch cubes—so we have to cut using a hand tool called a curd "harp." Resembling a musical harp, it has straight metal that are attached to a stainless steel frame. Carefully passing this through the coagulated mass will produce curds the size of walnuts.

For the harder Rupert cheese, in contrast, Peter uses the vat's automatic cutters set on a high speed to whack the curd down into pieces the size of corn kernels. This process takes ten minutes. Then the curds are stirred for an hour while being heated in the whey. Next, Peter uses a screen and, by running it through the whey, he pulls the curds together into a single mass. It resembles a giant albino sea sponge. At that point, the curd mass has to be hand-cut by a machete into huge chunks, then plopped into wooden molds.

Peter's virtuosity was on display the afternoon we received the distribution team from Provisions. He had no problem engaging them in conversation while groping under the surface of the whey with his hands, then using the machete to cut the curd "sponge" or mass into massive chunks. "Rupert is probably the cheese that's most fun for people to watch being made," Peter stated, cheerfully wielding his machete.

IF THERE'S ANYBODY WHO PERSONIFIES THE GROWTH— and growing pains—of the local food movement, it's Peter Dixon. Peter is one of the pioneers, and like the pioneers who settled the West, he has the arrows in his backside to prove it.

Even though Peter's father was a surgeon in Brattleboro, Vermont, "he always had to have a farm," the son recalls. Theirs was a small dairy farm in Guilford, Vermont, where Peter's stepmother, Ann, had started a business bottling and selling cow milk. (Thirty years ago, it was legal to sell raw milk in Vermont.) But the work proved too hard, and profits were elusive. So in 1983, in an effort to come up with a better value-added product, they asked Peter, nearly twenty-five years old at the time, and his brother, Sam, if they would join them in making cheese.

Peter was ambivalent at first. He was trying to make it as a musician. (Who wasn't those days in Vermont?) But that winter he reluctantly came to the conclusion that he probably wasn't going to be the next Jerry Garcia.

The Dixons started making Guilford Cheese Company Camembert and Brie, and within a couple of years they had developed a local reputation. Back then, there was no such thing as "artisanal" or handmade cheese. It was all called "specialty" cheese. (Even today our manufacturing license from the Vermont Department of Agriculture permits us to make and sell what they call "foreign-type" cheeses.)

Peter learned a lot in those early years. Unfortunately, most of the lessons were painful ones. In 1986, his family was introduced to a French cheese company that had ambitions of expanding into the American market—a common goal among European cheese makers at that time. They reached an agreement in which the French would provide the technical expertise, while Peter's family would build a creamery to the French partners' specifications (borrowing money to do so). In exchange for their know-how, the French were to receive a percentage of the royalties for ten years.

The arrangement ran into problems almost from the start. The master cheese maker who had been sent over to negotiate the deal wasn't the same person who returned to make the cheese. His substitute was a young guy—the boyfriend of the boss's daughter, according to Peter. Unfortunately, he wasn't experienced in making cow's milk Brie and Camembert. He had grown up on his family's farm making goat cheeses. The Dixons ended up with a lot of unsellable cheese, best enjoyed by the hogs on their farm.

But the larger problem was that Peter's family had borrowed

too much money to get the business off the ground—and the risk was all theirs. The French weren't required to contribute one cent.

Peter learned some valuable lessons from that experience, which he now passes along to the students in his classes (and which we've taken to heart). Call it cheese making 101: Grow in stages and, most important of all, let sales lead production. In other words, don't make cheese until you have a market for it.

The problem back in the 1980s was that there weren't enough markets. Artisanal cheese making was in its infancy. The infrastructure that supports the industry today—farmers' markets, retailers, celebrity chefs who feature it on their menus, television programs like *The Martha Stewart Show* that celebrate specialty producers and foods, and a cottage industry of food magazines— was far rarer back then and certainly hadn't reached a critical mass.

The Dixons reorganized with a new set of investors. They also hired Marie-Claude Chaleix, a legendary French cheese consultant who had worked on other successful cheese-making ventures in the United States, among them Coach Farm in Pine Plains, New York. She was able to develop excellent cheeses and, working side by side for a few months with Peter and his staff of three, taught them how to make top-notch Brie and Camembert. But even under Marie-Claude's guidance, the Dixons were being crushed under a mountain of debt they had accumulated from their earlier foray with the French. No matter how Peter's stepmother and Marie-Claude struggled to drum up sales, there simply weren't enough outlets for artisanal cheese. The new investors got cold feet and pulled out, and the Dixons were forced to declare bankruptcy in 1989.

Peter was understandably disillusioned and decided to go back to college. He enrolled at the University of Vermont, majoring in dairy food science. He now believes it was the smartest decision he's ever made. The chemistry and biology that Peter picked up at UVM proved invaluable, giving him an understanding of how cultures and yeasts work on a biological level and the ability to analyze and solve problems in the cheese-making process.

After Peter graduated from UVM in 1993, he got a job managing the creamery at Vermont Butter & Cheese Company, one of Vermont's largest and most famous cheese makers. It was there that he learned how to manage a large-scale cheese operation and integrate its various elements: production, quality control, food safety, and marketing.

That's also when he became a teacher. The company grew swiftly. When Peter arrived, sales were $1.5 million a year. When he left three years later, sales had grown to $4 million annually. (To put that in perspective, Vermont Butter & Cheese was making ten times the amount of cheese we make every day.) To achieve that growth required a small army of cheese makers, most of them trained by Peter. While this job helped him develop and refine his teaching skills, Peter was becoming more of a manager than a cheese maker. That role led him to the realization that he was happier working on a farm than in a factory.

But the knowledge and experience he had acquired those few years allowed him to market himself as a consultant and workshop teacher. The timing was perfect. It was just at the moment—in the late 1990s—that artisanal cheese making was starting to take off.

When Peter was still working as a manager at Vermont Butter & Cheese, he was asked to join a project run by the international development division of Land O'Lakes. Its goal was to help traditional farmers in the Balkans improve their standard of living by making aged cheeses. "I jumped at the opportunity," Peter remembers. His travels took him from Vermont to Albania and Macedonia, whose newly emergent governments were eager to establish a cheese industry, and where the milk he used to train his students sometimes arrived on the backs of donkeys. He helped farmers in Macedonia, whose cheese-making knowledge was previously limited to young cheeses such as feta. He did the same thing in Albania, helping cow farmers (mainly women) make more complex cheeses. Altogether, Peter visited Albania twice and Macedonia seven times and was in the region in 1998 when the shelling of Kosovo started. Refugees flooded over the Macedonian border, and he had to leave more quickly than anticipated.

In 2001, Peter had another entrepreneurial spurt. He started a cheese-making venture with a couple of farmers in his hometown, Westminster West, Vermont. He and his associates built a creamery and started making a line of certified organic cheeses, such as Asiago, mozzarella, and ricotta. They were sold throughout New England and established a solid presence in several Boston-area markets. But in 2004, Peter and his partners decided to call it quits for personal reasons.

Rust and I had taken a couple of Peter's workshops in 2001 and 2002. So when Ann Bridges, our cheese maker, left, we were thrilled when Peter came to work for us.

Peter is now in high demand as a cheese consultant, and he has an international reputation—his most recent travels have taken him to Shanghai. Peter's extracurricular activities are good for us, too—and not just because they help spread Consider Bardwell Farm's reputation; they also take the pressure off us to keep him fully employed during the slow winter months.

PETER'S GENEROSITY WITH HIS ENCYCLOPEDIC KNOWLEDGE probably has something to do with the communal nature of Vermont's cheese-making culture. That may also date to the hippie ethos of the 1960s, which is as much a part of the state as maple syrup, the Green Mountain Boys, and those Woody Jackson cows grazing peacefully on every pint of Ben & Jerry's ice cream.

Cheese makers such as Peter believe that all ships rise with the incoming tide: The more accessible cheese-making information is and the more people there are making top-notch cheese and succeeding financially, the faster Vermont will develop a national reputation as a cheese-making mecca, which will benefit everyone here.

Peter's enthusiasm as a teacher is what enabled us to ramp up cheese production from twenty thousand pounds in 2007 to thirty-five thousand in 2008. Our goal was to go a bit higher each year. Peter had personally trained all of our cheese makers: Margot, Leslie, and Chris. With Peter and this team, we would be able to keep the cheese room running at peak efficiency seven days a week if we wanted.

For potential employees, Peter's reputation and talent as a teacher are a definite lure. "He's so willing to share everything he knows, and he's a rarity in this country: people who know about small-batch cheeses," said Margot, who hopes to take that knowledge and use it someday to turn her family's cow dairy into a cheese creamery. "He could hoard his knowledge, but he's not like that at all. Teaching is his passion. He never makes you feel stupid."

The first time Margot made cheese by herself, she forgot to put the paddles on the blades that stir the milk and help the cultures and rennet disperse uniformly. The result was a stringy substance rather than the curd that results in good cheese. Another time, she forgot to close the valve that lets the whey drain out of the cheese vat. "He said, 'That's how you learn,' " Margot recalls. " 'You won't do it again.' "

My initial reaction to such accidents is to calculate the income loss. Peter, however, is so philosophical about it that I am immediately calmed. Someone a long time ago said that you can't cry over spilled milk. In our case, that's the literal truth.

Although Margot had never heard of Peter before she started working here, her father had. The veteran cow farmer had read about Peter in agricultural magazines and was impressed. "He said they charge a lot of money to go to courses taught by Peter,"

Margot said. "That got me excited about being here." We like to think that teaching young people cheese making is an extension of the apprentice system used for centuries in Europe to make traditional cheeses. It's like tuition-free graduate school in a little niche of food science.

Peter's generosity sometimes clashes with Rust's competitive streak. Rust grumbles and scowls when he thinks that Peter, the person most responsible for winning the medals Rust craves, shares our recipes with the rest of the world through his cheese-making courses. Peter, who studies Buddhism on weekends, just laughs off Rust's stinginess and diffuses any challenge from him with a sigh.

Rust's apprehensions remind me of the reservations expressed by Arrigo Cipriani, a client of mine and owner of Harry's Bar in Venice. I had persuaded Arrigo to write a cookbook, but it wasn't easy. He felt uncomfortable about sharing the recipes that his father, who founded Harry's Bar, had made famous and bequeathed to him. I explained to Arrigo that even with an explicitly written recipe, few can duplicate in the home kitchen the dish that a great chef has spent decades perfecting in his restaurant kitchen, but even knowledge alone shared by a master helps inspire people to take on something challenging.

The same holds true for Peter's fantastic cheeses. The recipe is not the key to fabulous cheeses; the magic happens when cheese-making techniques honed over decades are applied to high-quality milk—and done so by a person with expertise, passion, and dedication.

For the record, Peter claims he doesn't share our recipes. When he teaches a cheese-making class, he may teach his students how to make a tomme, the name given to a class of rustic, aged hard cheeses originally made in the mountainous regions of Europe. But he won't teach them how to make our tommes, Manchester, and Dorset. What makes ours unique, according to Peter, is the personality of the milk and the temperature and amount of time you cook it. But once again, a key factor is the milk. "When you're making raw-milk cheese," Peter says, "it's very hard to imitate anyone."

Peter's belief that he's not giving away state secrets also goes back to the idea of terroir—that no two cheeses, even using the same recipe, are going to taste identical because the composition of their milk will inevitably vary from one microclimate to the next. Other experts dispute this notion, but it is what Peter believes.

My own conviction is that only happy, healthy livestock produce the best milk. We take great pains to keep them clean, robust, and grazing on the best pasture grasses and forage. We move our herd every twelve hours to fresh, clean pastures, which are as free of manure and the resulting parasites as we can make them. We give individual attention to each goat, even as obsessive as naming them and teaching them to come when called. We shave them at the beginning of the summer to get rid of their thick, wooly winter coats and keep them cool, and we rigorously monitor their health. This is how good milk is produced, and it's my contribution to the cheese making and the prizes we win.

As a generalist and very nonscientific thinker, I take a somewhat hands-off approach to the cheese rooms at the farm. Although I've learned enough to know what artisanal cheese should look, taste, and smell like, and over the years I've assisted in making and aging all our cheeses, the daily job of crafting fine cheeses is not in my constitution. My attention span is short and getting shorter and I have to focus on other obligations on the farm, such as staffing issues, ordering equipment, paying bills, looking out for the goats' welfare—and then, of course, there's my literary agency. I dread to think how our product would taste if I were stirring the pot. Not only wouldn't we be winning any medals, but also I would probably have accidentally burned down the facility by now or sickened the entire population. That's why joining forces with a world-class cheese maker like Peter Dixon is the smartest thing we've ever done.

WITH THE PROVISIONS INTERNATIONAL STAFF WATCHING, Peter expertly cut the Rupert curd mass into pieces so precise that they fit exactly into four cheese molds, with little if anything left over.

However, for any cheese, turning the milk into curd and pressing the curd into molds isn't the end of the process. To paraphrase Winston Churchill, that's just the end of the beginning.

In the cheese vat, the curds and whey separate—but not completely. Another step, pressing, needs to be done after the mass emerges from the vat. The cheese is set out in molds made of food-grade plastic with perforations for draining out whey. Whether a three-pound wheel of Manchester or a thirty-pound wheel of Rupert, the soft, newly separated curds in their molds are topped by a weighted cheese press for two-and-a-half to three hours. Pressing ensures that any remaining whey will get squeezed out. The wheel is also taken out of the mold and flipped at least twice during pressing to produce a uniform shape. In the case of a thirty-pound bruiser like Rupert, that takes both strength and dexterity.

The reason we flip the cheese is so that the rind will grow smoothly and evenly. Most cheeses go into the brine room the following day. But in the case of a big, hard cow's milk cheese like Rupert, we wait two days to give the bacteria in the milk more opportunity to work their magic in a nice, warm environment.

Brining—placing the cheese in a saltwater solution—is important for several reasons. The solution, composed of water, salt, calcium chloride, and vinegar, slows the bacteria cultures down as they convert lactose to lactic acid, and it prevents contaminants from infiltrating the cheese. It also adds flavor and acts as a preservative.

Brining also starts the formation of the rind, which is the protective barrier around the cheese. Before the wheel goes into the brine, the outside of the cheese is still as soft as the inside, but after the cheese is removed from the brine, a hard layer, which feels similar to a shell, has formed around the outside of the cheese. This rind development is particularly important for cheeses that will age for two months or more, as it protects them during this maturation phase. In contrast, fresh cheeses such as Mettowee are lightly salted by hand, because they are eaten before it's necessary to have a tough, protective rind.

Cheese typically brines for about eight hours. But bigger cheeses can sit in the brine for as long as five days. That's the case both with Rupert and with Equinox, the newest addition to our line, which is essentially a goat's milk version of Rupert.

Cheese makers differ on how often to change the brine. Some never do. There are those in the Swiss Alps who attribute mythical qualities to their concoction. As Peter points out, if you keep your brine salty enough, it's virtually impossible for anything to grow or contaminate the brine. Besides, most Swiss cheeses tend to be hard, so it's less likely that chunks will break off and remain behind in the brine, risking contamination. We change our brine once a year, but we also send samples to a lab every three months to make sure it's free of contaminants.

Once the cheese leaves the brine, it goes into the cave to mature. This aging process, known by the French term *affinage*, can last for mere days or well past a year, depending on the cheese. What happens in the cave is crucial. When a cheese is first put into the cave, it tastes pretty bland. It's the aging process and the microbes that grow on the cheese and the enzymes they produce that give it its distinctive flavor.

Many small-scale cheese makers don't have their own caves. Hence the importance of operations such as Jasper Hill, which provide state-of-the-art facilities to such farms. But we have a ringer on our team: my husband, Rust. Unlike farms of equal size, we had the low-cost, high-tech know-how to build and maintain our own caves. We had two in November and a third in the works.

There's no ideal size for a cave. Some are as large as football fields. Our Dorset cave is a modest 8 x 20 feet, and our Manchester cave is slightly larger, measuring 8 x 32 feet. What's important is maintaining a constant temperature and humidity. The temperature should remain between 50° and 55°F, while the humidity level should fall between eighty-five and ninety-five percent, depending on the cheese type.

AS PETER WORKED THROUGH THE RUPERT PROCESS, HE maintained a running commentary. He also engaged the Provisions team in a discussion about the plummeting economy—which was approaching crisis proportions in October 2008—and what effect it might have on the cheese business. Provisions' marketing director, Chris Coutant, predicted it would have little effect. "When times get tough, food becomes even more of a comfort," she said. "When we're scared, there's nothing like sitting around a kitchen table with family. When you feel you have to curtail unnecessary expenses, people tend to eat out less."

Those might have been comforting words, except for the fact that a substantial part of our business is selling to restaurants. Many of our restaurant partners are fighting for their lives.

Meanwhile, consumers can sit around the kitchen table eating comfort food without spending $20-plus on a pound of cheese.

In response, we cut our retail and wholesale prices dramatically. As a result, appreciative retailers have been featuring our cheeses as their Pick of the Month or Consider Bardwell as their Farm of the Month.

Whatever the economy, Peter is confident that the local food movement is here to stay. "We've been on that path for a while," he says. "It's something that's going to be part of the fabric of our communities."

mating game

IN EARLY NOVEMBER, LOVE WAS IN THE AIR. WE WERE getting ready to put Boris and Kennedy, our two big daddies, into the milkers' barn to have their way with the girls. Truth be told, love had been in the air for at least a couple of months, judging by the behavior of both bucks and does, but we follow a common schedule of breeding in fall and kidding in spring. The gals had been twitching their tails urgently, crying out while facing the direction of the guys' quarters, and riding each other in frustration. Louisiana was the worst. She had apparently caught the bracing scent of buck at the heifer barn where we keep the boys, and stood for three solid days in the field below the barn, baying like a love-crazed teenager.

The guys were equally incorrigible. As Minny Buley put it in her inimitable fashion, "I don't like the bucks; they do unspeakable things to each other." Or at least to poor Tyrone, the smallest of the three. The other two bucks, Boris and Kennedy, had turned him into their "mate" until better options came along. Tyrone was becoming morose in October from the bullying. We worried he would become too depressed to be effective in his upcoming job, which was scheduled to begin on November 1. He even lost weight because the other two beasts shouldered him out of the way when their high-protein grain supplement arrived at breakfast and dinner.

Generous grain rations from August to November will help a buck build up his strength for the arduous job ahead. Once a buck is with the girls, he ignores his ration and is interested in one activity only. He paces, sniffing for signs of female readiness. A doe won't let a buck mount her until she knows she can conceive. That's a brief window of time: Does are in heat for only two or three days approximately every twenty-one days from late September through January. The jargon is that she won't "stand" for him until she's ready. So he frets and waits, and frequently tries anyway.

"They try to rub on me," Minny reported disdainfully.

"How can you resist a guy who French kisses?" I said of one of Tyrone's more adorable habits of trying to lick any innocent passerby.

"I'll like him again in the spring when he doesn't stink or pee all over his beard," Minny replied.

Bucks in rut have an unfortunate habit of urinating on their beards and front legs—a maneuver that's easier to visualize once you realize that bucks are rather well endowed with penises that, while pencil thin, can be a foot long. Dousing themselves with their signature scent is one way they make themselves irresistible to the opposite sex. While the notion of wetting oneself might not be an enticement to humans (not to mention the smell), female goats like it just fine. As a matter of fact, the bucks' overpowering aftershave, combined with the musk emitted by glands on their head, is instrumental in lighting the does' fire.

All of these signs were proof that the bucks were ready for action.

Tyrone's roommate situation had gotten so stressful that he actually broke out of the bucks' enclosure—twice—on one lovely mid-October Sunday. On the first occasion, I found him on the road trying to get at the milkers who were munching hay in their barn. I dragged him back to his own enclosure, about one hundred yards away, and made sure all the gates were securely locked. But then he broke out again. This time it seems he had found a place where the hay was piled high and used it as a ladder to escape.

Although I make light of Tyrone's prison breaks—he was really quite resourceful—it could have been tragic. The sex-crazed buck could have ended up in the middle of Route 153, which runs past our property, and gotten hit by a truck. Even worse, he could have caused an accident that injured a Sunday driver, for which I would have been liable. The possibility of someone getting hurt was horrific enough. Dealing with a lawsuit would have been a terminal drain on our bottom line.

Taking pity on the poor boy and to make amends for the bullying he suffered at the hands of Boris and Kennedy, I gave Tyrone a head start on the festivities. Two weeks early, we moved him to the Dry Pasture on the other side of the road, so named because it is hilly, rocky, and without a natural water source for drinking. There he had his pick of twenty yearlings. Imagine a manly man going from hard time at Alcatraz to having the run of the Playboy mansion: That was pretty much Tyrone's experience. I can't say whether goats believe in the sweet hereafter. But Tyrone undoubtedly thought he was being ushered inside the pearly gates, where he could have his way with a harem of the most gorgeous adolescent females in the land.

During mating season, we strap a harness onto each buck's chest. This holds a thick, uniquely colored cake of bright crayon. This year Tyrone wore orange, Boris yellow, and Kennedy green. When a buck mounts a doe, the crayon marks her hindquarters, proving the deed's been done and showing which particular buck had the honors. We can then keep records of the offspring's lineage and register the new crop of kids with the American Dairy Goat Association.

Needless to say, after a few days without any competition from those brutes Boris and Kennedy, Tyrone had firmly established a harem, and his self-confidence was fully restored. By November 1, a day before we put Boris and Kennedy in with the milkers, Tyrone, busy across the street, had already marked eight of his yearlings. Among his first conquests were Kerry, Lucia, Sophia, and Posey. On that fair afternoon, with the sun setting behind the hills, Tyrone set his sights on Daisy May. She seemed flattered by his attentions and was more than willing to become girlfriend number nine.

During the previous year's breeding season, I had been more concerned about which bucks mated with which does. I didn't want the herd to become too inbred. We haven't brought any does into our closed herd since the original eighteen, acquired in 2003 and 2004. All subsequent goats are their offspring, born and bred on the farm, and many were sired by Kennedy, Boris, and Tyrone. The main advantage of a closed herd is that you know everything about each goat. You know the goat's bloodline, and from that can guess whether a baby might become a productive milker because her mother and grandmother were, or whether an offspring might suffer health problems because her parents do. You can breed for attributes such as big udders and good milk production. You're also keeping the germs and parasites of other farms away from your animals. When new herd members are introduced to any farm, they must have accompanying vet certificates and are first kept in quarantine for about two weeks.

The disadvantage of a completely closed herd is that it becomes increasingly inbred. Over time, if we're not careful, we could see genetic diseases and bad traits creep into the population.

A livestock farmer must also be an amateur geneticist. Livestock with bad traits must be culled, leaving the stronger animals to contribute to the gene pool. Every season, we look at the offspring of the poorest milk producers or the moms who have weak immune systems, and we try to find homes for them outside our farm. They can become "brush hogs"—keeping underbrush at bay by foraging. And they also make fantastic pets.

Goat incest is inevitable. For example, when Boris and Kennedy are unleashed on the milkers, the girls include Boris's own mother, Nadia. If we were to discover that Nadia was marked with Boris's yellow chalk, we wouldn't want to keep her kid. (Having said that, I suspect that if Boris had gone after his own mother, she'd have given him a good, strong shove.)

Why wouldn't we separate sons and mothers and avoid the risk of an unfortunate encounter? I can't speak for other farmers, since they devise management practices that work best for their own farms. But the reason we don't is that it becomes a giant management headache once you start making exceptions and pulling healthy individuals out of the herd. Where are you going to put them? If one milking goat, such as Nadia, has to be isolated from her son, Boris, then the milking staff has to remember to find her and bring her into the milking parlor. Meanwhile, she would be very distressed about being separated from her herd and would probably suffer some stress-related illness. So we work with the situation. If she is bred by Boris, her son, and she has boys, then they will be raised for meat. If she has daughters, then we'll probably sell them.

Nadia's offspring had already proved to be somewhat disappointing anyway. They included Natasha, who suffered from medical problems all summer, and one of the baby goats that died of bloat last May. Nadia's yearling, Nanette, will kid this spring. We'll see what happens. Fortunately, this year Nadia was marked with green, so the sire of her offspring this breeding season is Kennedy, and she had boys.

I'm also less concerned about a little incest this year because we plan to keep just twenty doelings. They'll be the daughters of the best milkers, and I'll have more discretion about whom I keep and whom I sell or give away as pets. Our herd will have reached optimal size. All the yearlings across the street—Tyrone's harem—will join the existing milkers next spring. That means we'll be milking sixty-five does, compared to forty-five this year. Our goal is to increase the herd by approximately twenty does each year.

It already takes two hours to complete the milking. Given the capacity of our milking parlor, which has only fourteen milking stations, adding any more goats would turn milking from two-hour sessions in the morning and two in the evening to three hours at each end of the day. I already have enough trouble finding people to milk on weekends, with me as the milker of last resort. I'm often the one who does the honors on Saturday nights, when our teenage staff members have a hot date or head to a dance. And I'm there early Sunday mornings in the bone-chilling spring dawn, when Vermont forgets it's April, not January. But they are my goats, and the show must go on.

In 2009, the baby males will be managed by a young farmer in Dorset named Sara Cohen, who will raise them for meat. They'll stay with their mothers at Consider Bardwell Farm for a week or two, then Sara will take them to her farm, bottle-feed them for six weeks, and let them loose in her pastures to get big and strong. At four to six months, when they reach a weight of about sixty pounds, they go to slaughter. I'm glad Sara will be taking care of the boys; as I've mentioned, I still struggle with it.

Dealing with the babies is hard enough, but the bucks have been with us for a few years and I keep trying to prepare myself for when we'll have to replace shy Kennedy and Boris the silly bully to preserve the health of the gene pool.

But I don't think I could ever get rid of Tyrone. I adore him. When I told Minny that he's lovable because he likes to French kiss, I wasn't joking. How can a girl resist a guy who's that affectionate? Plus, Tyrone has great royal lineage: His grandmother Moisha was a showgirl from New Hampshire who was the 2004 National Udder Champion. That means Tyrone should pass along or "throw" (to use the animal husbandry term) some amazing udder sizes to his female offspring. One he sired in 2008 was Yoko, daughter of my favorite girl Koko. I'm sure that Yoko will become a star milker, if she's anything like her mother and grandmother. She's also the cutest girl in the whole 2008 class: champagne colored with black markings. Everyone is stunned by her looks and friendliness.

Although it's true that I've developed more pragmatic, farmer-like instincts toward our animals that complement my commercial requirements, I will still take back goats that I've sold or given away as pets if I hear that they're being ill-treated or their living conditions aren't up to my standards.

There was a case last August where I had to retrieve two goats

I felt were being poorly treated. I was tipped off by the cheese inspector, Greg Lockwood, who had arrived for a meeting at our farm and mentioned that he had spotted a couple of our goats in the road. The meeting was important, being about a potential new development: Jennifer Lawrence of Polymeadows Farm wanted to use our facilities on weekends to make yogurt. But I was too distracted by the idea of our goats being in the road to think about a yogurt business. I ran and got Amber Goff and Corey Chapin from the barn and dispatched them to find our goats. Luckily, though, Monty Post, a neighbor, had also spotted the animals when driving up the road, and he loaded them into his pickup truck and brought them to our farm.

A quick check in the barn showed that they weren't ours—or at least, weren't any longer. They were Rupee and Mabelle, the daughters of Ruby and Maple, born that spring, and I'd given them to a family who lived a half mile down the road and had three little boys. Each year we keep twenty baby girls and sell or give away the offspring of the least productive milkers, goats such as Rupee and Mabelle. That's also what we did with Flopsy, Lailani's undersized baby with the big personality. She'd bonded with Seth Haggerty, the sixteen-year-old son of Bill Haggerty, our DHIA milk meterer, on a visit to the farm in May 2008. So Flopsy went to live with the Haggertys on their farm in Sangate, Vermont. (By the way, her ears straightened on their own before she left.)

To get the family down the road started as goat owners, I had given them a manual on raising goats, along with some grain and hay. I'd even visited their house to make sure their fencing was adequate. They had a fenced-in backyard and had bought a giant dog kennel to house the girls, who were now approximately four months old. The last I'd heard, the family was having a lot of fun with them. These two girls were particularly friendly—which is how Monty was able to coax them into his pickup so easily.

As soon as the yogurt meeting wrapped up, I jumped into the car and went down to the family's house. By that time, Monty had returned the goats to them. I knocked on the door, but no one answered, even though I sensed that there were people inside. The little boys were probably home alone, I surmised. I knew their mother worked as a medical technician in Glens Falls, about forty-five minutes away, and got home around six o'clock.

So I went to Dutchies, the country store in West Pawlet, to do some sleuthing. The store owners, Will Kuban and Eric Swanson, were the ones who had originally told me about this woman—that she was looking for a pair of goats for her children. The men then updated me on the situation: Her husband had walked out on her shortly after she got the goats, the household was in chaos, and the store owners had heard that the goats kept escaping.

I felt a special sense of responsibility toward this pair of goats. Rupee and Mabelle were the runts of their litters, and when I gave them away, they were still so young that they were bottle-feeding. Naturally, I taught the family how to bottle-feed the babies—not just to relieve my staff from the burden, but also because I thought it would provide a richer bonding experience for the family. Having the children raise the animals from infancy would also build their sense of responsibility, I reasoned.

I went back to the family's house that evening. I explained that I wanted to be a good neighbor and felt uncomfortable interfering in her business, but I had to come talk to her because the two goats had been found wandering in the road.

"Yes," she admitted, "they've become a big problem." She said that her dog had apparently dug a hole under the goats' enclosure, which made it easy for them to escape. They would immediately head to the other side of the road, where they were attracted by the forage.

"Goats are escape artists," I explained. "My cheese inspector said he nearly ran into them on the road. I had people running up and down the street looking for them." (Not to mention having Amber and Corey out goat hunting, instead of doing their assigned jobs at the farm.) "They're either going to get killed or they could cause an accident, and the law says that you are liable. You could get sued."

She turned pale. "I'm sure you love them," I went on, "but don't you think it would be safer if I took them back, and you and your kids can visit them anytime you want?" I was trying not to be shrill. "I've got my car here. Why don't we just put them in the car, and you and the boys can kiss them good-bye." And they did.

The babies were terrified when I got them back to the farm. They'd been separated from their classmates for almost three months. As it turned out, Rupee was still tiny and had trouble fighting for food. Mabelle was slightly larger, but she didn't flourish either. By that time, both felt more comfortable around humans than among their fellow goats. Rupee, in particular, would follow me around like Mary's little lamb. So Sue Olsen, who managed the barn and the animals, always gave her special attention, and her assistant, Alex, basically adopted her.

As it happened, I knew a young New Jersey family who frequently visited their parents' weekend house in Dorset. They wanted a goat—but just one. They visited us over and over, asking for one. "No, no, no!" I said. "Two goats." Goats are herd animals and they'd be unhappy without a companion.

I called and told them that Rupee and Mabelle were available. I was thrilled and relieved when they agreed to take them both, confident that the pair had found a good home. I'd seen pictures of the family's home in New Jersey, and it looked well tended.

Now they send me pictures of the growing girls. In one photograph, Mabelle is being walked on a leash by one of their daughters. In another, the same little girl is feeding Rupee fresh hay. The most recent photo shows Mabelle looking right at home in an elegant downstairs room with parquet floors and French windows. I would doubt the authenticity of that photo, except for the fact that there's clearly a baby fence to keep her out of the living room. If only I could find good homes like that for every baby we can't keep.

BY THE AFTERNOON OF NOVEMBER 2, BORIS AND KENNEDY had scented themselves with extra cologne—and were ready to start speed dating. Margot and I put on coveralls and surgical gloves as a precaution, since we didn't want to contaminate our clothes or bodies with the bucks' overpowering musk, and we made our way up to the heifer barn. We also grabbed a couple of chalk harnesses.

Boris and Kennedy were happy to see us, though I can't say for sure whether they sensed what was in store. Maybe they just equated visits by humans with feeding time. In any case, they'd been living the bachelor life for seven long months and were now about to get sprung, going from celibacy to girls-gone-wild parties in an instant. For the next five months, they'd be living it up—until next year's milking season began and we isolated them again.

We keep the boys and girls together over the entire winter for practical reasons. It's easier to manage the herd if they're all in one place, and their constant proximity gives the boys an opportunity to breed any of the girls they might have missed previously due to the does' short cycle. Aptly, I call this winter breeding "cleaning up."

If I had any concern, it was that Boris and Kennedy would fight over the girls. But Jennifer Lawrence from Polymeadows told me not to worry. There is more than enough work to go around, she explained. Despite her sage assurances, however, the two bucks did indeed fight. They even broke some of the barn windows when smashing into each other during their initial excitement over the does and while trying to establish their harems. Eventually they settled down.

Come April, when the bucks are removed from the does' areas, the boys will start crying pathetically. By that point, the girls could not care less. The males will have served their purpose. From then on, all the does' energy and affection will be focused on giving birth, producing milk, and nurturing their young (to the limit we allow).

Polymeadows lets its bucks and over two hundred does mingle throughout the year. It makes little difference to them when their milkers get pregnant, give birth, and lactate because they milk for twelve months. We, on the other hand, "dry off" or stop milking our entire herd by late December. This gives everybody who works on the farm (me in particular) a breather from the twice-daily grind of milking. It's also more convenient when all your goats are on the same kidding and milking schedule. Finally, it's healthier to dry off a doe a couple of months before she kids, because milking places great demands on a goat's body and it's better for her to conserve as much strength as possible for her pregnancy.

IT WASN'T EASY GETTING THE HARNESSES ON BORIS AND Kennedy. Both are large and were excited. Male goats can weigh as much as two hundred fifty pounds and have thick, gnarly horn scurs. And boy, is that aftershave potent! Does are petite, about one hundred twenty to one hundred fifty pounds, and smell delightful by comparison.

Margot and I decided to go with the green chalk for Kennedy since the name Kennedy is Irish. Boris was assigned the yellow chalk. Then we leashed up Boris and led him down from the heifer barn to the field where all the girls were. They ignored his arrival, feigning indifference, as well-bred ladies do.

As a rule, bucks aren't big on courtship. They literally hit the ground running—as did Boris. But to give him his due, he also observed some social niceties, such as nuzzling his dates.

Not that he seemed especially picky. He started with the first gal who crossed his path. That happened to be Althea. The buck stuck his tongue out. That's supposed to be a turn-on, I take it, but it seemed to have little effect on Althea's libido. Then again, he might simply have been hoping to taste her urine stream, another step in the mating dance. Althea wasn't entirely unreceptive; she just didn't act horny, either—even after that bad boy kissed her hindquarters.

Boris would probably have had an easier time persuading Louisiana, the doe who earlier in the day had stood by the fence yelling "Yoo hoo!" in the direction of the heifer barn. But reaching Louisiana would have involved some problem solving, since she was grazing on the other side of a fence that divided the pasture in half, and the only opening was down by the far end of the field.

Whether or not Althea was in heat or just playing hard to get is difficult to say. The boys' interest in her suggested that she was, and she would eventually breed with both Boris and Kennedy multiple times in the coming days, according to Alex Eaton. I had charged Alex with keeping track of such things, so we could predict when a particular doe would give birth, and create a kidding schedule. (It's approximately five months after they get knocked up.) Alex estimated Althea's due date to be March 30.

Louisiana, in turn, was definitely waiting for her man. And love always finds a way. Leaving Althea in the dust, Boris discovered the opening in the fence and made a beeline to that damsel in hormonal distress.

In the meantime, Margot had fetched Kennedy from the barn and led him down to the pasture. Kennedy also went straight for Althea. There were about forty other milkers within feet, but they may as well have been invisible. Kennedy's luck was no better than his barn mate's, however. He quickly realized that Althea was playing hard to get and found his way around the fence to Louisiana, who hadn't yet committed to Boris and whose tail was wagging furiously. You know that old song "Shake Your Booty"? Well, goat girls dance to that beat. "Louisiana likes Kennedy," Margot observed politely from the sidelines.

Louisiana sniffed Kennedy's privates and apparently liked what she found, *because* Kennedy was riding her back within seconds. The act lasted no more than fifteen seconds. Nonetheless, Kennedy's first doe of the season was marked emerald green. Score one for the Fighting Irish.

But thanks to Tyrone's huge head start, Louisiana was the twenty-third doe bred overall. Tyrone had consummated his relationship with the yearling Nanette across the street as far back as October 21, and he'd had a bevy of other beauties since then.

With their coupling seemingly complete, Kennedy chivalrously still ran with Louisiana for a few more minutes. "He'll keep after her," said Margot, who knows about such things, having grown up on a farm. "He'll make sure the job is done."

And it's not as if Louisiana lost interest in Kennedy after their union was consummated. Even though she wouldn't give him the time of day twenty-four hours later when she was no longer in heat, she did spend the next few minutes nuzzling him, running her head along his flanks. Indeed, Louisiana even kept after him when it was obvious to everyone (except her) that Kennedy's attention was wandering in the direction of Daffodil.

Kennedy was crowned king of the barnyard, at least for that day. He bred three does: Louisiana, Daffodil, and Savannah. Boris wasn't heard from until two days later, when he impregnated Little Bea. The paternity of three does bred the following days—on November 4 and 5—remains in doubt, since both Boris and Kennedy took turns with them. But then Kennedy went on another streak over the following four days, adding thirteen milkers to his scorecard versus Boris's measly three. Boris answered with a vengeance starting on November 9, when he bred fourteen does over the next five days. Nonetheless, the single-day record rests with Kennedy, who made love to seven ladies on that Sunday.

By the latter part of November, almost all of the does were pregnant and a semblance of calm had descended on the barn. Tyrone had bred twenty-two does, Kennedy twenty-three, and Boris seventeen. Four young ladies—Stella, Pearl, Jasmine, and Althea—had dated both Kennedy and Boris, so the father of their children was destined to remain a mystery.

TWELVE

is anyone tasting
the cheese?

THE PLEASURES OF MATCHMAKING IN EARLY NOVEMBER were swept aside by serious problems later in the month. Zingerman's, an important cheese purveyor and specialty- food shop in Ann Arbor, Michigan, returned two hundred fifty pounds of the Manchester they'd bought through our Jasper Hill distributor, claiming it didn't taste the same as it had in August.

That was a painful, unexpected blow. Our precious, prize-winning cheese—rejected. It's like having your golden child with her 4.0 GPA and 800 SAT scores (or at least 750) rejected from her first-choice college. You take it personally, particularly when word spreads—as it invariably does in a small community such as ours. A friend came by the farm a few days later and said, "I heard you had a big recall."

In fact, there wasn't anything "wrong" with the cheese. We would still have been able to sell it without a problem at any of our farmers' markets and city restaurants. However, the returned cheese made us realize that there had been a major gap in procedures. This time, some of the cheese that made it into the caves, onto distributors' trucks, and into customers' hands was not up to the award-winning standards we had achieved and which I'd thought we'd been maintaining.

The highest hurdle to jump in developing a professional operation is consistency. If you expect to play in the big leagues, then top-notch retailers such as Zingerman's must be confident that your cheese will not only taste good, but will also have the same flavor profile from batch to batch.

It may seem as if consistency shouldn't be that hard to achieve. After all, if you regularly purchase some Gruyère, St. André, or Kraft Swiss at your local supermarket, you probably don't give a passing thought to its taste. You assume it will taste the same as it did last time. You expect that same flavor from year to year. That's why you return to it.

But there are reasons why big companies are able to maintain consistency while smaller artisanal creameries face more of a challenge. For starters, as Peter explains, the giant cheese producers remove a certain amount of cream from the milk in order to make sure the fat and protein ratio is always consistent. They also pasteurize the raw milk, thereby destroying at least ninety percent of the indigenous bacteria. Through these standardization and pasteurization processes, however, they may also lose the complex flavors associated with the activity of bacteria indigenous to raw milk, which small-batch producers tend to favor.

It makes sense for industrial operations to pasteurize their milk for food safety reasons, but for small-batch cheese makers like us who religiously police what goes into our goats' diet and continually test for pathogens, pasteurizing would be equivalent to killing the golden goose. The complexity of our cheeses, all those flavor notes, are a product of letting the raw milk sing.

"I hate pasteurizing," says Peter, our milk "whisperer." "I don't want to be around when it's happening. I can hear the milk screaming."

THE RISK WE RUN USING RAW MILK IS THAT ITS COMPOSITION changes from season to season and pasture to pasture, so we need to be on our toes to maintain consistency and quality.

There is an embarrassingly simple and effective method to reduce uncertainty: You sample the cheese at intervals during the aging process and give it a grade. The best stuff gets sold to distributors—and by "best" I mean cheese that doesn't suffer from excessive moisture or any other factor that might accelerate its aging process and make it overripe by the time it reaches faraway customers in Chicago or California. The rest can be sold at farmers' markets, stores, and restaurants closer to home, where you don't have to worry about lag time negatively affecting the cheese.

So had we been sampling and grading our Manchester cheese before Zingerman's rejected it? Sadly, no. This is one time Peter screwed up, pure and simple, and by his own admission. He described his failure to test the cheese as "a mental lapse." And it's true that it wasn't hardwired into our routine yet. In previous years, we hadn't been working with large distributors, but were mainly doing direct sales to farmers' market customers, cheese shops, and high-end chefs in the New York and New England areas. It was only when we started transporting cheeses long distances that these problems arose.

Peter's lapse traced back to early June, when we lost Debbie Tracy just as summer cheese production was set to start. Leslie, Debbie's assistant, tried to fill the void, but it took time for Peter to train her. Then Margot came aboard in July and had to be trained too. Naturally, novice mistakes were made along the way, as they are in any vocation. Perhaps they didn't squeeze out enough whey when pressing the cheese, or they didn't allow the bacteria or rennet to circulate evenly while stirring the milk, such as when Margot forgot to install the stirring paddles on one occasion, resulting in a syrupy mess. (The mishap was so blatant, however, that the cheese never made it out of the room, let alone onto distributor trucks.) And Margot said she saw the problems coming, because they were so focused on making cheese with all the milk that came in from not only Consider Bardwell Farm but also Polymeadows, Jersey Girls, and Noah's Arc Nubians. "We were just trying to get by in the summer and ramp up production," she explained.

WE REALIZED THAT THERE WAS ALSO ANOTHER FACTOR that negatively affected the taste of the cheese. Because we were making more than we were selling that summer, the cheese had piled up in our caves. Those aging rooms had become so crowded that air likely couldn't circulate efficiently, creating conditions that stimulated bacteria (the good kind) and yeasts on the rinds to grow more quickly. This didn't make the cheeses rancid or toxic; it just accelerated their flavor evolution.

Finally, we made quality control more of a challenge for ourselves by making so many different kinds of cheeses, nine in all, which are manufactured using different recipes and aged in different ways. Many cheese makers our size stick to one or two cheeses. But they don't have a presence at farmers' markets—an important source of revenue for us—where customers might ignore your booth unless you sell a variety of cheeses.

Our Mettowee, Danby, Manchester, Experience, and Equinox are goat's milk cheeses. Chester, Dorset, Pawlet, and Rupert are cow's milk cheeses. Our cheeses are soft and hard, fresh and aged, silver dollar–sized crottins of chèvre, and leviathan thirty-pound wheels of Rupert. Our washed-rind cheeses—Manchester (goat's milk), Dorset and Pawlet (cow's milk)—are literally bathed in a saltwater brine daily, weekly, or monthly, depending on the cheese and where it is in its aging cycle.

Then there's our Chester, the soft, buttery, cow's milk cheese that food writer Mark Bittman loved when it was served to him at Jean Georges, and that's known as a "wild rind" cheese. After getting bathed once when it goes into the cave, it's left alone except for a periodic flip. The cheese actually came about by accident. It started out as Dorset one fall morning in 2007, but the temperature in the cheese-making room was too cold, so the cheese didn't drain properly and contained too much moisture when it went into the cave. Because of this, black mold started to grow all over.

Peter and his team tried to get rid of the mold, but it just kept growing back. They brushed it. They tried aging it in a drier location. Nothing did any good. So then Peter decided to back off. Eventually, the mold disappeared on its own. The cheese also developed a distinctive appearance: Because it was so soft, the slats from the aging racks became imprinted on the rind, much the way a charcoal grill creates a distinctive grating pattern on a tender sirloin steak.

These grooves and the cheese's gray-green color inspired us to call it Turtleback, because it resembled the contours on a sea turtle shell. Eventually, our better marketing sense prevailed. Since Turtleback didn't evoke images of fine dining or gastronomic delight, we changed the name to West Pawlet Quarry. The rind reminded us of the color of the shale found in the prolific quarries in this part of Vermont. But Quarry didn't make it either. Finally, we settled on Chester, in tribute to Jersey Girls Dairy in Chester, Vermont, where all our cow's milk comes from.

Peter will never forget the first time he tried it. After sparring with it in the cave, then retreating in defeat, he brought it over to Sarah and Monty Post's home around Christmas 2007, after it had aged roughly sixty days. The three of them tried it, and their reaction was "Wow!" The greenish gray rind, which looked like the least appetizing part of the cheese, turned out to be delicious. It tasted something like walnuts, and the cheese itself was earthy, creamy, and redolent of mushrooms.

Chris Gray also had customers tast it, both wholesalers and at farmers' markets, and they loved it, too. This accidental newcomer has since become one of our most popular cheeses. But it's also one of the most finicky. The cheese needs to be consumed promptly: Because it's so moist, the flavor becomes too strong if it sits around the cave too long. As good as it is, we're not marketing it very much because of its perishability. Chester remains something of an insider's secret.

WE DID START TO SOLVE THE BACKLOG PROBLEM IN THE cheese caves in late August and early September after we signed up our new distributors, Cellars at Jasper Hill and Provisions International. The cheese wheels then started flying out of the caves. Peter also helped relieve the pressure by renting a cheese cave in Westminster West, where we shipped inventory of our three largest cheeses—Rupert, Equinox, and Pawlet—to age for six months to two years, thus freeing up precious shelf space in our caves.

We also instituted a new quality-control procedure in the wake of the Zingerman's recall: testing and grading all our cheese.

Grading a cheese begins by examining the overall appearance of the wheel. For example, Manchester, our aged mountain-style tomme, should have a uniform, rocklike appearance. It should be grayish or brownish in color, with touches of white, tan, or yellow, depending on the bacteria that's grown while it sat in the cave. If the rind is orange or pink and shiny, that suggests the wheel may have retained too much moisture; the color is produced by bacteria that thrive on the rinds when there's too little acid. This might present problems for our distributors, because the additional moisture suggests it's ripening too fast. The result could be a sharper taste than the wholesale customer anticipated.

After Peter examines the wheel's overall appearance, he'll extract a "plug" or sample of cheese using a tool called a "trier." During this process, he'll note how firm the cheese feels as it's penetrated by the trier. Then he'll examine the texture of the plug, looking for cracks and gas bubbles, which can result either from the goats' diet or from flaws in the cheese-making process. Ideally, the cheese will have few of these. However, gas bubbles, cracks, or excess moisture don't make a cheese inedible. We've been selling cheese like that all along, and often to rave reviews and to outlets like Murray's and Artisanal in New York City, who turn around and sell it without complaint to some of the finest restaurants in the world.

Finally, Peter will taste it. If the Manchester is good, it will have a nice, classic flavor: clean and a little spicy. A poor batch might display an orange rind, have a mealy texture, and taste unusually strong. Before the cheese goes to market, Peter together with Margot, Leslie, and Chris—an informal jury panel—will repeat the tasting process and they'll enter the information in a notebook and on a computer. That way they can assess the outcome and decide whether a particular batch is more appropriate for sale at farmers' markets or through distributors.

Our grading system is pretty simple. We have three categories: The lowest grade is "poor," which means the cheese isn't worthy of our farm's name and is discarded. The next grade up is "market" quality. It doesn't fit the ideal flavor profile of that cheese. There's nothing wrong with it, but it may be ripening too fast. That means we'd want to sell it at farmers' markets before it becomes overripe. The final category is "distribution" grade. That's the cheese that goes to our far-flung national customers through our distributors. It fits the ideal in terms of flavor, texture, and uniformity. It also tends to mean it's on the mild side. But that doesn't mean it's better or worse than market-quality cheese, only that it will still taste the way it's supposed to when it reaches the table of some consumer in the Midwest or Napa Valley.

ALL CHEESE IN THE CAVE—YOUNG AND OLD, WASHED AND unwashed—gets turned at least once a week. That's to expose all surfaces of the wheel to the air in order to equalize the conditions in which it ages. If the wheel isn't turned, moisture could collect along the bottom, making it moldy and, in the worst cases, mushy.

Turning cheese, and working in the aging room in general, can be either deeply meditative, moderately boring, or border-line unbearable, depending on the kind of person you are. Un-like the cheese-making room, which is bright, airy, and a hive of activity, the aging room is like an isolation chamber—quiet, with low claustrophobic ceilings, and smelling of ammonia, a by-product of the aging process caused by a breakdown of the protein. "You do a lot of thinking," Margot said. "The work you're doing is pretty mindless, so you let your mind wander— besides the fact that you're choking on the ammonia stench."

Each person develops preferences regarding the "care and feed-ing" of certain cheeses. Margot is partial to Manchester, while Leslie has a soft spot for Dorset. Nobody likes taking care of Pawlet, a creamy, Italian-style toma. But that has less to do with the cheese's taste than its relatively cumbersome ten-pound size and hard-to-reach location on cave shelves.

A visit to Jasper Hill back in July led to some serious cheese room envy. Making the pilgrimage were Margot and Alex, neighbors Sarah and Monty Post, and Peter. The operation is impressive, starting with its vista of rolling hills. Jasper Hill co-owner Mateo Kehler provided a guided tour through the cheese-making facilities, showing us how fresh, warm cow's milk goes straight from the animals to an adjoining cheese room, which sparkled in the bright afternoon light. It's here that the Kehlers and their staff make their celebrated Constant Bliss, which tastes as rich as triple crème, and Bayley Hazen Blue, a natural-rind blue cheese. Then we toured their state-of-the-art caves: seven of them built into the side of a hill.

Originally, the Kehlers' dream was to help save Vermont's family-owned dairy farms by helping farmers diversify into value-added products such as cheese. But since the entry cost can be so high, the Kehlers also found ways to ease farmers' financial burden by taking over aspects of the process, such as aging, distribution, and marketing.

If certain female members of our staff got misty-eyed during the tour, it wasn't just because of Mateo's sweeping vision or macho good looks. Rather, it was because of his practical innovations that are making cave work easier on his employees. His cheese racks are on wheels (ours are not), so instead of having to strain to reach the more remote wheels of cheese, you can simply spin the racks around. He's also developing machinery that will partially automate the aging process, flipping the cheese wheels at regular intervals so humans don't have to.

TO RELIEVE THE POTENTIAL TEDIUM OF THE CHEESE room and cave work, Chris bought us a high-quality satellite radio to keep the staff entertained and distracted. Unfortunately, differing music preferences occasionally trigger culture wars. The person who arrives first usually decides the day's audio selection—at least until a coworker can't take it anymore and demands a change. Margot, for example, likes the intellectual patter of National Public Radio. Leslie prefers country music. Peter is into classic rock.

"I can't stand it," nineteen-year-old Leslie says of NPR. "It's just people talking. It's boring."

If the chatter weren't bad enough, the political subject matter during 2008—an election year—only seemed to deepen the liberal/conservative divide among employees. There's a lot of down time in cheese making, with long stretches spent standing around waiting for the milk to coagulate. And there are close quarters, in both the cheese room and the caves. This is the kind of environment where beautiful friendships can develop or differences can fester.

Young Minny Buley was a McCain-Palin supporter, as well as an avid hunter. She admitted that her thoughts turned to vandalism every time she passed Margot's Toyota Corolla in the barnyard, which was plastered with a collage of liberal bumper stickers and "Obama for President" signs. "I walk by it every day and it drives me crazy," Minny admitted. "If I had a permanent marker, it wouldn't be good."

The underlying fact is that, despite their occasional conflicts and ideological differences, our young employees are all incredibly proud of what we're doing and proud to be a part of it. They see the farm praised in the newspapers and in high-profile magazines.

They also get real satisfaction out of being a member of the team. And their friendships don't end when they leave the farm for the evening. During the summer of 2008, Peter, Margot, and Alex would all go to Sarah and Monty Post's for potluck dinners several nights a week, with Peter and Monty playing music late into the evening. (Sarah, a fourth-grade teacher who was thinking of switching careers, worked in our cheese room making Mettowee during the summer of 2008. Monty, a musician and artist, hauled Polymeadows milk for us.)

The local kids who work here came to the farm already as friends (one recommends the other), and they have a great time, even if the work is more than occasionally down and dirty—such as mucking out pens. For some reason, the most fun they have all summer occurs when the first- and second-cut hay arrives in July and August. No matter where they work on the farm—whether in the barn, in the cheese room, or out in the pastures—they rush over to help. One person throws the hay off the wagon, while a second takes it and tosses it onto the hay elevator; inside the barn, a third farmhand picks up each of the bales as they come off the elevator and throws it to two or three others who are stacking. In two hours, they might stack a thousand bales of hay weighing almost fifty pounds each. With all that teamwork, it's like an orchestra in perfect sync.

IN NOVEMBER, EVEN THOUGH WE QUICKLY INSTITUTED quality-control procedures, our problems with Jasper Hill lingered. We discussed their concerns about the consistency of our Manchester and the possibility of selling them Manchester as "green" cheese, letting them age it in their own caves. Nonetheless, Mateo paid the farm another visit in December to help us understand his concerns. While tasting sample batches with Peter and his team, Mateo described some of it as tasting of "bile."

I was having a hard time with the situation even before he made that comment. The week after Thanksgiving, the two hundred fifty pounds of cheese that Zingerman's had returned to Jasper Hill, and which had been held in the original cardboard cartons for several months in the distributor's storage, arrived back at our farm. I was upset, and not just because I was the one who had to unwrap the wet, sticky wheels and find cave space for them. I also knew they were most likely too overripe to sell, even at local farmers' markets. Eventually, we donated the whole lot to a neighbor's pigs.

I was even more disturbed when Mateo suggested a follow-up visit, one that would include Marc Druart, cheese technician at UVM's Vermont Institute of Artisan Cheese. Mateo wanted to make cheese "with our girls," explained Chris, who was acting as go-between. Peter, in his Buddhist mode, had taken the original criticism about the taste of the rejected cheese in stride. But this time he put his foot down. As mild-mannered and nonconfrontational as Peter is, he issued something of an ultimatum. If Mateo showed up with Marc, "I'm out of the picture," he said. "The cheese room is my realm. I know everything they know, and I don't need their help."

I agreed. Mateo might as well have said he wanted to look through my closets. It felt like an invasion of privacy and an insult to Peter, who, having just turned fifty, had been making cheese for thirty-three years and had the national reputation and accolades to prove it. I also hated the fact that Chris, who manages our customer relationships very skillfully, was—between trying to keep an important customer satisfied and taking my heat about getting Mateo to back off—was caught in the middle. But I made it clear to Chris that Peter, not Mateo, was our cheese maker and any further discussions concerning our relationship with Jasper Hill would have to include him.

Peter also made a good point: Instead of pinning our hopes on Jasper Hill to help us build a national reputation and worrying about pleasing stores in the Midwest and California, we should focus our energy on markets closer to home.

Our relationship with Jasper Hill would survive in the months after we improved our quality control and held our ground about not being supervised. Mateo skipped the planned visit with Marc and he agreed to continue selling our aged cheese rather than set up a system of purchasing green cheese from the brine room to age at Jasper Hill. I know that Mateo really is looking out for Vermont cheese makers' best interests, and I respect what he and his extended family have accomplished, both as cheese makers and as marketers, in a relatively short period of time. I'm also aware that Mateo must protect his multimillion-dollar investment in his caves and distribution company. Fortunately, by protecting himself, he's also protecting us. Nonetheless, the episode rankled. At the time, we were stretched financially and sorely in need of income.

PUTTING THE JASPER HILL EPISODE IN PERSPECTIVE— it probably had to happen. I should have been paying more attention. And I should have thought through our growth plan: I would have realized that in ramping up production while using only one veteran cheese maker and several novices—no matter how hardworking and well intentioned—something had to give. I should have asked the question, "Is somebody tasting all the cheese?"

Perhaps I was blinded by the validation of our business that those shiny silver medals seemed to provide. Maybe I was guilty of hubris, thinking I could juggle my work as a literary agent and goat cheese farmer. Peter had been distracted, but was the managerial incompetence on my part? There seemed to be a communications breakdown, and the ultimate responsibility for that rested with me. Hard mistakes, hard lessons. I got the message. Now we're all more careful. And we have all learned to taste and grade cheese.

THIRTEEN

trimming trees and costs

THE STRESS OF OUR QUALITY-CONTROL PROBLEMS WAS EVEN more acute in the context of the almost daily recession headlines in December, about thousands of job cuts, industry stalwarts like General Motors and Bear Stearns requiring bailouts or going under, and the Dow dropping 700 points in one day. I was convinced that our business was in jeopardy and obsessed over how to cut back on expenses in order to get through the coming months. To give myself a little peace of mind, I tried to embrace the coming holiday; I looked forward to the Christmas party we hold every year at the farm in early December, one of the few, if not only, times all the employees are together and can celebrate.

This year we held it on December 15. Everyone gathered in the farmhouse living room. We had a big fresh Christmas tree that twinkled with clear lights and rose-glass orbs. I made lasagna, mac 'n' cheese, and other warm, comforting, aromatic dishes. Leslie's mom, Margot, and Sarah Post all made holiday cookies. Monty Post brought champagne, Peter dandelion wine (so good, but also so unexpectedly intoxicating). With holiday music playing softly and candles glowing throughout the rooms, although not a fanciful, formal party, it was magical.

That is, until Leslie hit me with a bombshell in the middle of the party.

"Did you hear that I quit college?" she announced brightly.

She said that she was planning to drop out of Adirondack Community College, where she was studying criminal justice. Her new plan was to work for us full time. The only problem was that paying her for full time wasn't in my projected budget.

A few days earlier, Leslie had apparently gone to Peter Dixon and asked if she could take the cheese-making certification course at UVM's Vermont Institute for Artisan Cheese. Getting certified is a recent trend: Students take two five-day courses that cover milk chemistry, hygiene and food safety, starter cultures, cheese chemistry, and other topics.

I want our team to have opportunities for advancement, but standing there at the Christmas party listening to this news, I was upset. For starters, Leslie and Peter might have consulted me as well—especially since I was expected to pay for the course. But it was more than that. The Christmas party was supposed to be a temporary respite from the pressures weighing on everyone at the farm. For those few hours, we were supposed to be one big happy family, with me as den mother—or that was my fantasy. At the very least, I wanted the party to be a reasonably successful social experiment, where local teenagers like Leslie, Minny, and Amber, ambitious college students and graduates like Corey Chapin, Margot, and Alex, and talented professionals like Chris, Peter, and Rust could come together to celebrate our collective contributions to award-winning cheese.

I tried not to dwell on Leslie's announcement and instead immersed myself in the Christmas party spirit. It *was* almost possible to forget about the financial challenges and the cheese production problems of recent months. Together we could simply enjoy some good food and the spirits that Monty and Peter had brought.

But I discovered that people were still talking about Leslie and there was one thing that everyone agreed on, be they barn or cheese people: They all thought she was making the right decision by dropping out of college. It was similar to the path that most of them had traveled.

Peter had taken thirteen years off between the time he started and finished college. Sarah Post had taken two years off from college and worked at a fish cannery in Alabama. Both Alex and Margot took a gap year between high school and college, and Margot fondly remembers living in Belgium, learning to speak French, and gaining twenty-five pounds eating chocolate.

191

When I shared my feelings with Leslie—that at her age, education should be her most important concern—she didn't accept my advice in the caring spirit it was given. "Why do I need to waste any more time on criminal justice?" she demanded, her voice rising.

I said, "There are other things you can study."

Leslie said, "Alex went to college, and now he's milking goats." Alex, too smart to join the spat (and undoubtedly aware that careers don't get much more respectable these days, even chic, than raising healthy goats in a culture increasingly attuned to the importance of safeguarding the nation's food supply), kept his feelings about Leslie's slight to himself.

I really do believe in the value of a college education, but my most immediate concern was the additional costs I envisioned. Of course, it's my farm and I could tell Leslie that her decision didn't work with my budget, but Leslie was a good cheese maker, and I also didn't want to create ill will with an unpopular decision.

THE ONE PERSON WHO AGREED WITH ME THAT LESLIE shouldn't quit school was Chris Gray, because he, too, was thinking about the financial impact of additional expenses. Chris didn't see how we could pay anyone to work full time when there was neither enough work to fill their hours nor money to cover it. Business was so weak in December that I wasn't sure where I was going to find the money to keep people working, let alone increase Leslie's hours and pay.

Shortly before the Christmas party, Chris had shared with me a cash-flow chart showing revenue for the current year and forecasts for the next; he was clearly alarmed.

Sales had plummeted by fifty percent in November from the two previous, strong months. Even worse was that December was usually a blockbuster time for cheese sales because of office parties, Christmas dinners, and New Year's celebrations. But this year, the Christmas orders were light. Provisions International told us their distribution business had taken a nosedive at Thanksgiving. Jasper Hill wasn't ordering from us either. They still had one hundred wheels of unsold Manchester sitting in their caves from earlier shipments.

The winter months are slow under the best of circumstances. After the holidays, people stay home to take off the weight they put on at Christmas and New Year's and to undo the damage they did to their credit cards. We count on the money we make in the run-up to the holidays to help tide us over until spring, especially since we stop milking in December. Our only income comes from the inventory we have stockpiled in our caves.

Consumers were clearly making adjustments to save money, and that effect rippled through the retail chain.

When I attended the December farmers' markets in Vermont, I could see that shoppers' bags had virtually nothing in them. People were looking and tasting, but they weren't buying. I wasn't convinced by the argument that comfort food would hold its own during the economic crisis when people stuck close to hearth and home, as Chris Coutant, Provisions' marketing director, had suggested in November. Not in light of the reports coming back from farmers' markets that lower-priced cheeses, such as feta, were becoming increasingly popular.

It looked as though we would be losing money almost as far as the eye could see. When I saw Chris Gray's projections for 2009, I seriously questioned whether we could survive the economic downturn. What was the point of being in business if we were in the hole between $1,500 and $3,500 per week through next July?

So in early December, we started counting pennies and making difficult decisions. As small an operation as we were, I knew that we were literally supporting four farms: our own, Jersey Girls, Polymeadows, and Noah's Arc Nubians. We weren't milking anyway, due to the downtime in the goats' cycle. But I spoke with Lisa Kaiman of Jersey Girls Farm to warn her that she might have to find other buyers for her milk. (I knew she would at least be able to sell to Agri-Mark, the dairy cooperative she'd been supplying before she signed up with us.) I also met with Polymeadows and told them that in the worst-case scenario, they would have to dry off their herd—in other words, stop milking, because we wouldn't be able to buy it.

Fortunately, Peter still had business as a consultant to new creameries. It was encouraging to see that the economy hadn't killed people's dreams of becoming artisanal cheese makers. He agreed to work only one day a week in the cheese room, so Leslie could have more hours.

Even Chris Gray, a partner in our business, had to change his modus operandi. To cut transportation expenses, I told him that there was no need for him to stay at the farm during the winter work weeks. He should remain in the city, manning the farmers' markets and trying to drum up new business. I would drive the cheese down to Manhattan every Monday when I returned to the city for work.

DURING THIS TIME, WE WOULD TRY HARD TO BOLSTER OUR relationships with East Coast retail stores, both large, formidable operations like Murray's Cheese and smaller outlets like Saxelby Cheesemonger, a diminutive jewel of a shop at the Essex Street Market on the Lower East Side of Manhattan. These stores had dedicated, knowledgeable customers, and at holiday time that's where the action is. That's also where I wanted Chris to be—servicing existing customers and awakening potential new ones to the delights of Consider Bardwell Farm cheese.

When you look at cheese that's invitingly stacked in cases at Murray's, Saxelby, or other great cheese vendors, you'll often find evocative little description cards. "The aroma is that of fresh cut grass and asparagus stalks, and the flavor is deeply mineral and sweet," Anne Saxelby wrote of our Manchester. These store notes are great tools for the consumer who wants to know what he or she is buying. But most shoppers never stop to think about the cost, effort, relentless uncertainty, and insomnia-suffering farmer behind a good cheese. I guess they shouldn't have to.

Fortunately, Anne Saxelby has that insight. Part of what makes this whole odyssey worthwhile are people like Liz Thorpe at Murray's and Anne. They understand the obstacles to success in this business and the many components that have to align themselves correctly for a cheese farmer to succeed. In the case of Consider Bardwell Farm, that includes an owner who's crazy enough to believe this work would be rewarding and too driven or deep in the hole to throw in the towel when it's not (which is at least half the time); an outside source of income to help bankroll the dream; a ringer like my husband to do the building and repair; a talented cheese maker at the top of his game; a professional marketing person; young people who are willing to work hard for not much more than minimum wage; a healthy goat herd; and a certain amount of dumb luck.

But the cheesemonger herself is a vital part of the equation. She or he is the connective tissue between the farmer and cheese maker in the rural depths of Vermont, Wisconsin, France, or beyond and the foodies in New York, Chicago, or San Francisco. She's between the teat and the table, if you will. Her role may be even more pivotal than those selling other premium-priced products—whether diamonds or high-end wines.

I don't mean to disparage the good salespeople at Harry Winston or Sherry-Lehmann, New York's most famous wine shop. But I doubt they bring the same sense of mission to their vocation that people like Anne Saxelby or Liz Thorpe or *maître fromager* Max McCalman do. Part of it is that American artisanal cheese makers constitute a very small community. For Liz and Anne, the product they sell is about more than cheese. They might be motivated to support locally grown food, sustainable agricultural practices, and saving the planet. But all the cheesemongers I've talked to acknowledge that, even more, it's about an emotional connection to the food because they know the people who make it. Anne and Liz have likely visited almost every farm whose cheese they sell. They're intimately acquainted with the backstories: This one is a painter; that one used to work for IBM or GE before chucking it all to become a farmer.

Anne has told me that from what she has seen, the number of people who are born and bred dairy farmers is very low. She's fascinated by farmers' life stories and how that informs what cheese they make.

As important as it is for us cheese farmers to have someone capable of knowledgeably representing our product to the public, I believe it's just as important for people like Anne, Liz, or Max to represent a producer they know and like and whose practices they believe in.

It's an exaggeration to call Saxelby Cheesemonger a shop. It's more like a nook off the entrance to the Essex Street Market. The market had been established in 1940 by Mayor Fiorello La Guardia to get food peddlers off the overcrowded streets. Anne's space is all of 120 square feet, with a 23 x 23-foot display case and a 7 x 6-foot walk-in refrigerator. But that's a good thing, according to her.

"Whatever fits, fits," she has said. "It forces us to choose carefully which cheese makers to work with. None of the cheese ever languishes. That locker gets filled and emptied out every week and a half."

If so, it's not just because of the quality of the cheese, but also the effervescence with which the twenty-seven-year-old proprietor sells it. Anne has been to our farm twice. The first time was in 2005, when she came to visit a friend who had left her job at Murray's Cheese to intern on the farm. Anne's most recent visit occurred this past June, when she organized and led a paid cheese tour, dubbed "Day A-Whey." About twenty cheese aficionados came for a weekend of communing with goats, cheese-making workshops with Peter Dixon, and some cave action.

To me, the most astonishing thing about the event was how much people were willing to pay for the privilege of socializing with Lailani, Koko, and company: $750 per person for a shared room, or $900 for a single at the Dorset Inn. Of course, the price included a guided tour of the farm and a picnic lunch, provided by me, plus a four-course harvest dinner on Saturday night at the Dorset Inn.

But Anne's passion for cheese certainly predates her visits to our farm. Like me, she grew up loving cheese indiscriminately. "Super-aged cheddar was fine," she says. Her horizons expanded when she visited a friend in Florence one summer and saw the cornucopia of cheeses being sold at the city's central market. When she returned to the United States, somebody suggested that she check out Murray's. She did, again and again. "I was stalking the people at Murray's," she recalls. "I was the person who tried twenty-eight cheeses and bought a quarter pound of each thing."

Her stalking turned into a 2003 summer internship at Murray's, a bustling but unadorned emporium on Bleecker Street in Greenwich Village, followed by a six-month cheese-making apprenticeship at Cato Corners Farm, an award-winning family-run cow cheese farm in Colchester, Connecticut. When she returned to Manhattan, Anne became a full-time employee at Murray's. But she knew she wanted to start her own business and eventually make cheese herself. So she went to France and apprenticed for three different cheese makers in the Loire Valley. How many salespeople at Harry Winston or Sherry-Lehmann go into the trenches like that?

Anne developed an understanding of the European craft of cheese making and also sympathy for American cheese makers trying to compete in the same league. The Europeans have hundreds of years of experience on us, as well as a cheese-making infrastructure and government subsidies. Nonetheless, when Anne returned to the United States, she knew what she wanted to do: open a shop, and not just any shop, but one dedicated exclusively to American farmstead cheeses. To this day, it remains the only one of its kind in New York City.

She was inspired, at least in part, by a trip to Paris and a visit to Fromagerie Marie-Anne Cantin, the legendary cheese shop on the Rue du Champs de Mars, in the shadow of the Eiffel Tower. "The shop impressed me so much," Anne remembers. "The cheese was displayed like jewelry. Gorgeous window displays, with different sizes and colors."

She also liked the French concept of small shops dedicated to selling only one or two things well, and she particularly admired the Parisian shops La Maison du Miel near the Madeleine, which sells only honey, and Mariage Frères in the Marais, dedicated to exotic teas. In Cantin's case, the selection was cheese, yogurt, and a little fresh dairy.

As good as Europeans are at making cheese, Anne knew from her stints at Murray's and Cato Corners that some American cheese makers are just as talented. Still, she had her doubts about whether consumers would support a shop devoted solely to farmstead American cheese.

Then in 2006, fate intervened. Robert LaValva, a leader in sustainable agriculture, told Anne about a tiny space that had become available at the Essex Street Market. She took the leap. Although any new business is risky, Anne could take comfort in knowing that the gamble with this storefront could not have been any smaller, literally, it being a teeny counter and a walk-in cooler.

Business was slow when she opened in May 2006. "It was a total uphill battle," she recalls. The Lower East Side neighborhood was "transitional," as they euphemistically say. Much of the street traffic was methadone addicts who frequented two clinics in the vicinity; needless to say, they provided no walk-in sales.

But slowly, business picked up. Publications such as *Time Out New York* wrote about Anne—what's not to like about a bubbly New York University graduate trying to save the planet one chunk of cheese—or free-range egg or dollop of luxurious crème fraîche—at a time? And the neighborhood did start to change. More hip young families moved in who would frequent the store, happy to accept a free piece of cheese for their toddlers to teethe on. The business began to grow through word of mouth. On a recent morning two and a half years after its opening, Anne had a steady stream of customers, all stylish young women who came in to buy a loaf of bread or some eggs (Anne sells forty-five dozen a week), then got tempted in the course of their conversation with Anne to purchase some cheese as well.

By living at Cato Corners Farm (whose owner, Elizabeth MacAlister, used to be a social worker) and then getting to know other cheese makers over the years, Anne has noticed certain recurring themes: Most cheese makers started out with profitable jobs on the side or savings to support their cheese-making habit. And many were searching for meaning in their life, which their prior careers had failed to provide. Part of Anne's success is that she impresses upon her customers how each cheese is a unique creation, the result of an indescribable alchemy that occurs when you put driven Type-A personalities together with lactating livestock.

Anne believes that American cheeses are quickly catching up to those produced in Europe. "In the United States, there's still a lot of bootstrapping: people cobbling bits and pieces of information together," she acknowledges. "But I think there are some gorgeous cheeses being made here that are just as good or better."

She enumerates a few, such as those made by Laini Fondiller of the organic Lazy Lady Farm in Westfield, Vermont. In addition to being delicious, her cheeses exhibit Laini's sly sense of humor. One of their best sellers is Barick Obama, a double-cream cow's milk cheese in the form of a brick. Another is Fil-a-buster, a truly stinky cheese that's an apt commentary on the U.S. Congress.

Anne and Liz Thorpe of Murray's Cheese entered cheesemongering from different directions. Anne started out as a studio art major who decided she wanted to become a businesswoman. Liz began as a businesswoman, then decided she wanted to be an artist, or at least do something more creative than just make money. After graduating from Yale in 2000, Liz became an investment banker at Goldman Sachs, jumped to an Internet startup during the technology bubble, went to work in ad sales for CNBC when the bubble burst, and then decided to reassess her life. "I thought it would be interesting to learn about something really random," she says. "I liked cheese."

Like Anne, Liz's quest led her to Murray's Cheese. The evolution of this cheese shop during her years there is a good barometer of the exploding interest in sustainable agriculture in general and artisanal cheese in particular. "When I started, there were eleven people," remembers Liz, who came aboard in 2002. "I was the only woman. Most were Spanish-speaking men in their forties, with a couple of hipster guys thrown in. It was very different from the way it is now. We have sixty-five employees, eight departments, and more women than men. A lot of career changers and people with college educations."

Liz has watched how American cheese has made rapid strides, and consumers, especially in urban markets such as New York, have become more educated. She says, "I went to my doctor, and he said, 'That Humboldt Fog is one of my favorite cheeses.' I thought, 'Wow! Times have changed.'" Humboldt Fog is a bloomy-mold ripened goat's milk cheese from California that has won top honors from the American Cheese Society on several occasions.

Unlike Anne, Liz still thinks American cheeses have a way to go before they can compete with the best European cheeses. "Are there American cheeses that are as good? Yes. Better? Yes. If I were to make a plate of the best, most delicious cheeses in the world, American cheeses would be on that." The difference, she adds, is that "Europeans have got it down. Their cheeses are *always* delicious and in balance. That's true for any great European or American cheese. I've had a lot of American cheeses that were great once. Three other times they were mediocre. A truly exceptional cheese is great every time you taste it. That's truly hard to find."

That has been our problem. Then again, we've only been at this for six years, not several hundred. And some of the better-known Vermont cheese makers, such as Vermont Butter & Cheese and Grafton Village, don't have the distraction of raising their own goats or cows. "You add farming, and it's like having two jobs," Liz acknowledges.

Or three, if you add my literary agency.

When I started, I wanted a farm. Then I wanted animals to populate that farm. Then I wanted to make a little fresh chèvre. Then I got in over my head.

But I've had enablers and coconspirators. When I hired Peter, people warned me that his cheese-making dreams were at least as bold as mine. They said he would pressure me to ramp up production. He has, and we did.

We now make nine different kinds of cheese, whereas many other cheese makers focus their energies on perfecting only one or two. Mateo and Andy Kehler at Jasper Hill, for example, make four: Constant Bliss, Bayley Hazen Blue, Windemere, and Aspenhurst.

"It's easier for people who make one cheese to be consistent," Anne has said. "Peter is brilliant, but he makes his job harder because he's making so many different kinds of cheese. If you focus on a few you do really well, it's going to be a lot better for you and your customers in the long run. But I also understand that wandering, restless spirit that Peter has. You want to try different things."

But we also feel that maintaining variety is key to staying afloat. After all, we've seen how essential that is at farmers' markets, where profit margins are more attractive. Customers want both hard and soft cheeses, premium cheeses such as Manchester, and more affordable, everyday cheeses such as chèvre or feta. If they see only two or three cheeses on the table, they'll walk right by.

It's nice to see that both Liz and Anne remain remarkably upbeat about their own prospects during this economic downturn, partly because they truly believe that they're part of something bigger. Though Anne acknowledges that sales to restaurants have dipped, she thinks the general trend remains the same: People are thinking more about where their food comes from, especially in light of recent food-safety scares.

"They're starting to think about what kinds of foods they're buying and why," she has told me. "People might opt for a smaller amount of a small farmstead cheese instead of going to Whole Foods and picking up a big anonymous wedge of something."

She's weathering the storm. "We're making money. We're paying ourselves, even though we're not rolling in cash," Anne says. "If I'd wanted to do that, I wouldn't have sold cheese. We're small, and our overhead is low. We're just lucky, because that allows us to focus on what we want to do."

Liz counts American farmstead cheeses as one of those "affordable luxuries." A wheel of Chester is far more doable than a new Mercedes or Caribbean cruise. She also sees the recession as a cultural moment, a time similar to the post-9/11 era when people take stock of their lives. She thinks this should be good for the long-term prospects of farms like Consider Bardwell. Anne agrees, adding that people want to feel confident about what they're putting in their bodies.

But I also believe there's a more intangible element to it, a fulfillment of fantasy. You can see it at play when people come up to you at farmers' markets in New York City: They're buying more than cheese. When they purchase a piece of Manchester or Rupert, they're buying a connection to us farmers and a vision of goats grazing on emerald Vermont fields and drinking from running brooks. We're their surrogates, living the life many of them aspire to. They don't realize what an exhausting and expensive life it is. But that's okay. Their candied visions are included in the price of the cheese.

Tapping into such dreams, Liz is now writing books. Her first as coauthor was *The Murray's Cheese Handbook: A*

Guide to 300 of the World's Best Cheeses. Her next one, *The Cheese Chronicles*, which I agented, is a more personal book, "a journey through the making and selling of cheese in America, from field to farm to table" as its subtitle says. She's a beautiful writer.

Anne Saxelby's ultimate goal is to have her own farm. "I'd make goat cheese," she said. "I like goats quite a bit. They're mischievous little buggers."

OUR MISSION AT CONSIDER BARDWELL FARM ISN'T JUST making great cheese. It's also raising happy, healthy goats. And there's a third goal: creating an environment where our employees—especially the younger ones—want to work and might even pick up some good habits that will serve them well in the future. I'm too insecure to think of myself as a role model—Lord knows I've made enough mistakes in my life that I'm not sure I'd recommend my path to anyone else—but I'd like to think that Leslie, Minny, Ciara (my goddaughter), or Amber might be able to look at me and see that you can accomplish more than you think if you believe your destiny lies in your own hands and have the accompanying work ethic and focus.

And they do have good habits. We're lucky, because our teen workers invariably rise to the occasion, mustering the discipline to show up at 5 A.M. to milk the goats or work on weekends, even though they're going to school and may be holding down another job.

I don't think I've ever seen kids who work harder than these girls. Amber couldn't attend the Christmas party because she was working at AJ's that evening. It's one of those places where the locals do a double take when someone new walks in.

One night when I was there with a friend, we ordered burgers, and, knowing that Amber was manning the grill, asked the waitress to send our compliments to the chef. Amber came out in the navy hay-flecked sweatshirt I'd seen her wearing in the barn earlier that day. I suppose a little goat in your meal isn't so bad.

At Christmas, I gave each of the teenagers $100 out of my own pocket. Chris received a new computer, and Margot and Alex were given $50 gift certificates to the Northshire Bookstore plus a couple of my favorite books. I also unexpectedly found a way to give the girls the Christmas present they'd wanted most: more work hours. On January 2, when I walked into the cheese room where Margot and Leslie were working, they told me that Sue Olsen, our barn manager, had just quit.

"She said she was going to email you," Margot informed me.

I can't say I was surprised, even if I was slightly hurt that she hadn't told me face-to-face. Sue had started working for us only last spring, and in recent months she'd been working fewer and fewer hours. It wasn't just because the barn activity slows down after we dry off the does. The teenagers relayed that Sue had told them she didn't need the income.

I liked Sue. We had similar entrepreneurial work ethics. But I also liked the idea that there was a female working on the farm who was at least close to my age. Sue was about to turn fifty. I thought we'd be able to talk in a way I couldn't with anyone else on the farm, with the exception of Laura Fletcher, who was only here during kidding season. But it didn't turn out that way. Sue worked hard, but she kept to herself. The most unequivocal proof that we never bonded was that she hadn't even let me know she was quitting. She said she'd email me?

"She said if you were ever in a pinch . . ." Margot said.

"I like having an old lady around," I said wistfully.

"So Margot and I were thinking . . ." Leslie said. In the next breath, we were talking about how Sue's departure created opportunities for the rest of the staff to work more hours.

Sue actually returned a few days later, but only to pick up her final check. While there, she told me she would come back any time I needed help. "I didn't really *quit* quit," she said. "Margot and Leslie seemed to want more hours."

"They made it sound like you quit," I said. But I just let the subject drop.

We were entering a period of deepening economic anxiety, and I was happy to trim expenses any way I could. Soon enough, Alex Eaton started assuming more and more of Sue's responsibilities, doing morning and evening chores. I had been trying to find additional work to keep him busy: I also had him create a kidding schedule and even put him in charge of planning the communal vegetable garden we were going to plant next spring.

Producing more of our own food would help us keep costs down. We also bartered and shared more with our farm partners and friends. Between milk, cheese, and meat from the goats; veal from Jersey Girls Farm; and the cornucopia from the garden— potatoes, tomatoes, lettuce, squash, beets, broccoli, beans, peas, and lots of herbs—we were preparing to ride out the recession, or the next Great Depression, if things kept getting worse.

FOURTEEN

guests at the farm

CHRISTMAS IN VERMONT BROUGHT A HOUSE FULL OF guests. It's unusual these days to have every room occupied by friends, as happened habitually on Shelter Island. But it was an important time for me to have laughter and chatter through the house and even hear people comment on how delicious Consider Bardwell Farm cheese was. Even I admitted that I needed a break. And it was nice to have the reminder that we made good cheese.

For most of the week between Christmas and New Year's, we hosted my daughter, Sam, and her Italian boyfriend, Davide; our friends Mary Murray and her husband, graphic artist Craig Jordan, who designed our attention-getting farm logo—a simple, appealing image of a handsome, self-confident goat painted red against a black background—and cheese labels; and their daughters Oonagh and Ciara.

I stayed in Vermont the full week before Christmas to prepare for my guests, buy and wrap gifts, and shop for meals, rather than hunker down as usual in my midtown office in Manhattan on the far West Side. I had waited until the last minute to shop and looked for creative, economical presents. I bought everyone $50 gift certificates at the Northshire Bookstore in Manchester Center, Vermont, the most accommodating, warm, and wonderful bookstore on earth. As I love goats and cheese, I love authors and books. Cheese and books are both crafted, tangible, enriching reflections of their source. I'll always love both. It's important to me to support books and the struggling publishing industry, which has supplied me with a decent livelihood all these years.

I also bought tons of little gadgets and mementos at the Family Dollar Store in Granville. Rust and I gave Samantha, a public school teacher in New York City, money to spend as she liked, and we presented each other with flat-screen TVs for both the farm and the city, purchased in part with our American Express rewards dollars. At Mary Murray's suggestion, I gave her children mittens, slippers, and scarves and bought her husband *John Lennon: The Life*, Philip Norman's latest book. I was Philip's editor at Simon & Schuster when we published the definitive book on the Beatles, *Shout: The Beatles in Their Generation*.

I made a very modified version of the Italian Christmas Eve meal, which consists of seven seafood dishes: I stopped at three—

shrimp, salmon, and scallops. Davide, whose family owns a hotel on the island of Elba, where he and Sam met last summer, loves to cook and ended up making a pasta dish with the salmon.

The young couple were rather touchy-feely during the entire vacation, much to the disgust of thirteen-year-old Oonagh. She confided to her mother that she would never behave that way if she had a boyfriend.

Having a working farm means doing chores even on Christmas day. I bundled up in layers for the trip to the frigid barn before the children woke and scuttled back before they could rip open their gifts. But as harsh as conditions were outside, it was nice to share some holiday cheer with the goats.

I skimmed over the icy barnyard (more and more carefully as I age) and distributed hay and fresh water in all the feeders and buckets.

Goats appreciated my little doses of TLC, like the warm water I put in their buckets twice a day when temperatures were below freezing. They loved it when I sang to them, and my rendition of "Jingle Bells" made them excited and attentive, if perhaps slightly baffled. They probably responded to the fact that I sounded like a goat bleating. I also did "Jingle Bell Hop": Tyrone climbed up the side of the hay feeder and craned his neck, pushing his head and lovely beard in my direction for a Christmas kiss.

On Christmas afternoon, Mary, Sam, Davide, and I walked for several miles on the property. We trudged over ice-encrusted fields and rolling hills tinted amber by the setting sun. The hike challenged Davide, who wasn't used to hill climbing or the Vermont cold. By 4:30 P.M., it was getting dark and the wind was whipping up the snow; it was time to head home and start cooking Christmas dinner.

We were having a ten-pound filet mignon from Lewis-Waite Farm. I'd swapped it for a ten-pound wheel of Pawlet at the Dorset Farmers' Market just after Thanksgiving. We had salad, roasted potatoes, green beans, roasted Brussels sprouts, and a fruit tart made by Sam and me. Our neighbors Pippa and Michael Katz came and brought an entire dinner of turkey, stuffing, and English white sauce. Because Michael had been under the weather at Thanksgiving, he wanted to have the whole Thanksgiving experience along with Christmas. Pippa, much to Michael's horror, forgot the cranberry sauce.

Nonetheless, it was a terrific meal with good people. Gift enough for me.

BEFORE WE OWNED THE FARM, I USED TO THROW DINNER parties at the drop of a hat and hosted an annual Christmas holiday party at our Manhattan apartment. In those days, entertaining had been second nature, rather than the distraction from farm work that it has since become. On any given weekend, we would average six houseguests in our Victorian white elephant on Shelter Island. To keep track of the endless parade of visitors, Rust and I had a New Year's ritual: We would buy a calendar specifically to keep track of all the weekend guests we were going to invite the following summer. But we also wound up having a lot of last-minute arrivals—and we welcomed them.

Rust, contrary to his ornery demeanor, loves company. He likes to entertain and hold forth. He's just not inspired to do any of the prep work for entertaining. He won't even go out and buy a quart of organic milk. (Under duress, he'll hit Price Chopper for the cheapest possible deal.) On the other hand, he is happy to drive several hours to airports or train stations to pick up guests.

Toward the end of my time on Shelter Island, we would have an August fortnight when we'd host as many as twenty Europeans, including many of Rust's old colleagues from architecture school. But I always seemed to have a decorating project going, which thwarted guests from using the rooms undergoing makeovers. Fortunately, we had two stories of wraparound verandas that provided additional space, and friends could always be found lounging in hammocks or sitting on the wooden steps to the garden with cups of tea balanced on their kneecaps.

Rust would wander from group to group telling stories, sharing memories of architecture school, and offering tours of his architecture job sites. He usually had several projects going on Shelter Island and a couple in the Hamptons—and still does.

Rust's family would come in May—at least five or six strong—arriving ahead of the summer heat and humidity. We would go through boxes and boxes of tea. A "cuppa" may be a joke here, but it's a serious ritual with the English.

The "rellies" have come to Vermont only twice, but they've significantly improved our quality of life. Rust's sisters, Peg and Joyce, planted a garden alongside our Danby marble terrace. In two weeks, the two English women transformed a brown mess of weeds into a spectacular garden. All summer, it's crowded with lupines, delphiniums, lavender, sage, savory, bridal wreath, ice plant, hens and chicks, ajuga, and chives. Our snow geese love it and climb in to have a munch now and then. The birds hail from Shelter Island and were transported to Vermont by Rust in his van. He thought they'd appreciate the freshwater ponds of Vermont as much as Long Island's saltwater inlets, and they do.

Having a less-demanding social life in Vermont was part of the plan. When we bought the farm back in 2001, I didn't want it to become a resort destination the way Shelter Island had. Part of the reason I fled Shelter Island was to get away from the relentless social scene. (Little did I know there'd be people living on the farm 24/7, or anticipate the cheese tourists who would stop by from midmorning till sunset—including several hundred on one occasion when we were listed on a farm-tour weekend without our knowledge.)

As the years go by, we have had fewer and fewer houseguests, mostly because I'm too busy to entertain. In the summer, I'm running the farm, milking goats, stacking hay, and manning farmers' markets. In the winter, it's frigid cold, and Rust's British penchant for keeping the thermostats painfully low deters all but the hardiest adventurers. My idea of the perfect houseguest these days is someone who knows how to entertain herself or who's happy to come up and do all the cooking, like Sharon Bowers, one of the partners in my literary agency.

One particularly intrepid couple, Pam Krauss and Jim Bradford, have been here twice—once in the winter before the farm took over all of my energy, and once last summer during farmers' market season. Pam not only cooked for us, but also dressed up in a milkmaid's frock and sold cheese at the Dorset Farmers' Market. A natural-born shill. At dinner the previous evening, her husband had offered to help me with chores before we went off to market. He didn't know that we'd have torrential rains during the night that would flood the milkers' pen and leave a stinking mess of manure, urine, wet wood shavings, and wasted hay. Jim got an insider's view of the romance of farming when we got up at 5 A.M. to scrape down the concrete floors and collect the debris for pickup. I could not go off to a farmers' market knowing that the barn was smelly and that tourists might visit and think us sloppy. Jim never complained—but I did, a lot. When we finally made it to the market, I parked myself on a cooler and dozed off while Pam hawked our cheese.

Pam is a top editor who had an unprecedented four cookbooks simultaneously on *The New York Times* best seller list that Sunday morning—with TV cooking stars Rachael Ray, Giada De Laurentiis, Ina Garten, and Martha Stewart. But she thought it was a treat to sell cheese at a Vermont farmers' market. Go figure.

ALTHOUGH I REPRESENT MANY CHEFS AND FOOD LUMINARIES, I have been reluctant to invite them to spend the weekend in Vermont. I just can't see worldly, sophisticated chef-restaurateurs like Jean-Georges Vongerichten or Arrigo Cipriani waiting in line to use the downstairs shower, or brushing their teeth with our sulfuric-smelling tap water. It's hard to imagine having Jean-Georges whipping up his glorious turbot with Château Chalon sauce or Arrigo his *risotto con seppia nera* (risotto with black squid ink) on the old stove I inherited from my daughter.

Our friends who do visit understand that along with hospitality they might occasionally find a hole neatly cut in the ceiling that's patiently waiting for Rust to install a new chimney, or wires hanging out of walls that are waiting for sconces that we haven't even sourced yet. It always takes longer than it should, but every domestic effort comes second to paying for farm equipment and ensuring that cheese-room projects are completed.

Given all that, it's surprising to realize that Consider Bardwell Farm is edging a good deal closer to completion after a mere eight years than our Shelter Island Heights place was after fifteen. As of late, the improvements have been coming fast and furious. We didn't have a working bathroom when we bought the house in 2001, but now we have three (or five, if you count the bathroom in the smithy and the one Rust installed in the barn over the summer, by popular demand).

Perhaps these could have been done sooner, but Rust also still maintains his full-time job. When he's up in Vermont, he has more pressing demands on his time: Building cheese caves takes precedence over designing and building a new kitchen, especially when the old one works just fine. When we first moved in, I hired a contractor recommended by Chris Kimball—a pal and founder of *Cook's Illustrated* magazine and creator of PBS's *America's Test Kitchen*—to make radiator covers and paint the walls, floors, and kitchen. But Rust does the majority of our plumbing and electrical work—when he gets around to it. Our beautiful Italian-made shower is a case in point. Purchased for our downstairs bathroom, it has been sitting in the garage for the last two years. For a while, I attached a picture of the new shower to the side of the existing moldy one, with its anemic water flow. My hope was that Rust might get the message. I also wanted to signal to our guests that better times were just around the corner. But after some time, the photo got tattered-looking, too, and it didn't spark Rust into action, so I eventually took it down.

Our water-filtration system is another case of delayed gratification. Rust bought it for me for Christmas in 2007. (Isn't he romantic!) Its purpose was to remove the smell of sulfur and anything else that happens to come bubbling up through the pipes. Unfortunately, it's still sitting under the sink, hooked up to nothing.

Then there's our fabulous new combination fireplace and wood-burning stove in the dining room. This was meant to heat the whole house this past winter. But in September—the very weekend Rust planned to install the final pieces—the milking system broke down and Rust was forced to make that unanticipated trip to Canada to buy a new motor. On the positive side, the fireplace is in position, so we no longer have a hole in the dining room wall. It looks quite good, even if it's not working yet. Geoff Miles, Rust's assistant, spent a weekend here in the late winter, helping Rust cut holes in the ceiling to run the flue through. But they are forced to wait for warm weather to extend the chimney through the roof. If we're lucky, the job will be done and fire roaring by July or August when it is 90° outside.

SOME CHEFS WHO DO VISIT MISTAKE OUR PERENNIAL STATE of chaos and disrepair for "charm." Mark Bittman came up in August 2006 and stayed in the smithy for three days. As writer of *The New York Times* "Minimalist" column, Mark's specialty is creative, simple, delicious food. But I suspect that even Mark was out-minimalized when he got a look at our very basic cooking facilities. Maybe that's why he spent most of his time grilling outdoors.

Mark has also remained at arm's length when it comes to our cheeses. He told me from the start that he couldn't write about Consider Bardwell Farm cheese in *The New York Times* because of the conflict of interest, which I certainly understand. As his agent, I wouldn't want him to compromise his integrity and jeopardize the trust of his legions of readers. My coauthor, Ralph Gardner, also couldn't write about us when he did a piece for the *Times* on urban professionals who go into farming. (I wonder where he got the idea.) The one time Mark made an exception, in a *Times* travel piece about local foods and restaurants in Vermont in December 2008, I kind of wished he hadn't.

He described the cheese list at Hen of the Wood, one of his favorite restaurants in Waterbury, Vermont, as high quality, but then added about the cheeses, "They have a way to go before they reach the levels of complexity displayed by the European originals on which they are modeled." He then went on with the parenthetical sentence: "(I'm reluctant to single any out, since at least one is made by Consider Bardwell Farm, co-owned by my literary agent, so I would get in trouble no matter what.)."

Despite the faint praise, such is the clout of *The New York Times* that the Sunday that the piece appeared, business was especially brisk at our stand at the Tompkins Square farmers' market on the Lower East Side, with people who had read Mark's story asking for our cheese. I also got a lot of positive feedback from friends and clients, who'd say, "I saw that your cheeses were mentioned in *The New York Times*!" I guess the saying is true: As long as they spell your name right, any publicity is good publicity.

ANOTHER HOUSEGUEST AND CLIENT WAS SUVIR SARAN, A wonderful chef who fuses Indian and American cuisine. He's the author of *American Masala* and co-owner of Dévi, an upscale Indian restaurant in Manhattan. Suvir visited with Raquel Pelzel, a food writer who coauthored his book and has since become a good friend and client of mine. On his first visit here in the summer of 2004, one of the dishes he whipped up was crisp tortilla chips with chickpea and yogurt, a wonderfully crunchy, spicy-hot Indian salad. That weekend, they helped me bake and serve at the Fish and Game Café. Suvir, an experienced chef and restaurateur, was appalled by our café's unlicensed kitchen. He stayed busy washing everything in sight.

In fact, Suvir and his partner, Charlie Burd, became so enchanted with the farm that in June 2006 Suvir asked if Charlie could come up and spend the summer. He would help me with farm management, farmers' markets, and so on. I didn't know Charlie, and Charlie certainly didn't know me, but I leapt at the chance to have an additional pair of hands. He would live in the smithy, so he could have his own space and privacy and I could have mine.

Even in jeans and a T-shirt, Charlie was an impeccably groomed urbanite. He was clearly out of his element, but worked hard and was a smash hit with our teenage farmhands, who'd never seen anything quite like him. On one memorable occasion, wearing a country bandana rakishly tied around his head, he hoisted his six-foot frame to the top of the hay wagon to toss bales down to the teenagers who were loading them onto the hay elevator. All of a sudden, he furiously exclaimed that he'd broken a fingernail. That provoked howls of laughter from his country audience. They could never quite grasp the idea that he would travel to New York City once a month for a manicure-pedicure.

However, the situation proved problematic for me. Neither Charlie nor Suvir could stand anything that wasn't picture-perfect and orderly, and Charlie kept suggesting ways he could help move things along. I've noticed that this kind of passion for perfection is something most great chefs have in common. In contrast, Rust and I flourish—or at least feel unthreatened—living in controlled chaos. Our lives are permanently "under construction."

Fortunately, Charlie and Suvir found a more suitable outlet for their organizational genius when they bought their own picture-perfect farm about six miles away in Hebron, New York. They not only acquired goats, but also sheep, llamas, guinea hens, and heirloom chickens. They manage it all while entertaining lavishly, filling their farmhouse and fully fitted guesthouse with visitors from far-flung places.

FIFTEEN

sell, cut, or perish

THE PLUMMETING ECONOMY EXPLAINS WHY CHRIS GRAY could be found manning the stand at our newest farmers' market on a frigid Friday in January 2009. It was in Manhattan on 97th Street, between Columbus and Amsterdam. "It's the 10th Mountain Division of cheese selling," said the perennially cheerful Chris, even though customers seemed as scarce as IPOs in this frozen economy.

January is not the most hospitable time for outdoor shopping. Nonetheless, that month we increased the number of farmers' markets we attend to compensate for the loss of income from restaurants and distributors. We were anxious to find new sources of cash anywhere we could.

Ironically, our business plan (such as it was) had called for the wholesale business to sustain us through the slow winter months. But the opposite was happening. Retail was our mainstay. Because we had no choice, we began to participate in five winter markets in New York City alone. Two were brand-new: the Friday morning market at 97th Street on the Upper West Side, and the Brooklyn Flea Market in Dumbo, the hip waterfront neighborhood that looks out on the Manhattan skyline.

We also participate in weekend markets in Rutland and Dorset. This being Vermont, you can buy things there like hand-knit mittens and postmodern birdhouses, and listen to troubadours play guitar while you purchase fresh bacon and first-class cheese. Those markets are indoors, but their spaces are unheated. With temperatures hovering in the twenties, they may as well be outdoors. We also do a market each Saturday in Westchester County, New York, alternating between Mamaroneck and Briarcliff Manor.

On that wintry Friday morning on the Upper West Side, Chris found that most of the commercial activity centered not on selling but on bartering. Due to the dearth of customers, Chris and his fellow vendors were doing brisk business trading cheese, winter greens, apples, and other products. "It's one of the few perks of doing this," Chris explained. "You eat really well."

An actual customer meandered over to buy our feta, which we call Danby. Over the summer, there had been a great debate at the farm about whether or not to make feta. Even though farmers' market customers often asked for it over the years, it wasn't until this summer that we had enough milk to spare. It also wasn't very attractive from a financial standpoint, because we couldn't sell it for as much as we do cheeses like Manchester and Rupert.

But our thinking changed when faced with a surplus milk supply and caves crowded with unsold cheese. Among feta's charms is the fact that there's no maintenance. It ages in a five-gallon bucket of brine for a couple of months without much tending.

With customers now cutting corners, feta has become one of our best sellers. A half-pound container in brine costs $8. That's $16 a pound, compared to $24 a pound for Manchester. It's also a natural for farmers' markets, where people buy fresh greens and then ask themselves, "What cheese goes well with a salad?" It's also a practical choice for customers because it's essentially pickled, so it keeps in the refrigerator almost indefinitely.

Feta is a favorite with outdoor cheesemongers as well, especially during the winter months, when one's fingers don't work so well. It comes already cut, weighed, and stored in a plastic container, so it doesn't require the slicing and hand-wrapping of each purchase. We also like how it attracts a new customer base. Economically minded shoppers who might have once walked away when they heard our prices now buy something. You've made a new customer, and the next time around, they might be open to purchasing one of the more expensive cheeses.

That's what happened with Chris's feta customer. She had bought feta at the previous Friday's market and reported that her family was so impressed, she came back for more. "It passed the Greek mother-in-law test," Chris announced.

During their transaction, Chris persuaded her to try some Rupert, proclaiming it to be near the peak of perfection. "Butterscotchy and very dry, with a nice crunch to it," he said. "At six months, it was good. At ten months, it's like someone stepped on the gas."

How can you resist a pitch like that? She bought a half pound.

If retailers such as Anne Saxelby play a pivotal role in educating and winning over consumers, the farmers' market cheesemonger may be even more important to consummating a sale. The two are slightly different figures. Ask Chris and he'll tell you that representing a farm at a teeming market like Union Square or Tompkins Square Park in Manhattan is almost a form of performance art. No one wants to hear a slick sales pitch, but there are certain rules of the road. Even if you repeat the same lines over and over, you have to find a way to make them sound genuine, personal, and say them with a big smile on your face. You're always standing up; you're never sitting. You lean in toward them and make sure you establish eye contact. At the Vermont markets, you say, "Where do you live? Are you visiting?" You practically ask them how their children are. In New York, whether or not they remember your face, you say, "You look so familiar. Haven't I sold you cheese before? Which of our cheeses have you tasted?" And they say, "Where is the farm?" "West Pawlet, Vermont," you answer. "Vermont?" "Yes, I'm so happy I got to come down here." They look pleased that you're excited to be let off the farm. If you can engage them in conversation, they're always going to buy something.

It's not unusual for customers who have developed a relationship with the farmers' market cheesemonger to drop by the farm, often unannounced—whereupon they are likely to be slightly disappointed. Although we do have beautiful pastures, adorable goats, and a comely team of cheese makers, Consider Bardwell is still a modestly funded working farm in a rural setting. The roads are rutted, the barns are perennially in need of fresh paint, the equipment has seen better days, and manure is hard to avoid.

There are also time-management issues. "People have this expectation of sipping lemonade on the front porch and having all the time in the world to chat about cheese and goats," Adirondacks farmer Sheila Flanagan told Ralph Gardner for his *New York Times* piece on urban professionals who made a midlife switch to farming. Sheila is co-owner of Nettle Meadow, which makes Kunik, a wonderful triple crème cheese. "They think it's a great, quiet existence. They don't realize it's an eighteen- to twenty-hour day to do this."

I'll second that! But the cheesemonger is the personification of that better, cleaner, healthier lifestyle. It's remarkable how many farmers' market customers confess their ambition to buy a few goats one day and make their own cheese. The cheesemonger knows better than to destroy those fantasies.

Relationships develop at these outdoor stands. Over time Chris gets to know many customers personally. He can recite their cheese preferences and, more importantly, their children's cheese preferences. And you start out with a hidden advantage over the guy in the next booth selling, say, broccoli rabe. Cheese is a fun food. It makes people smile. And those smiles, week after week, make your day—especially when the temperature is below freezing.

If Chris isn't manning our stand himself, customers are disappointed and want to know where he is. Doing business with such a passionate and personally invested seller adds value to the transaction, so customers know they are getting more than just food for their money; they are making a tiny investment in a food producer who cares.

Customers assume Chris to be an expert on all things cheese. They may tell him they're having four people over for dinner and drinking Riesling: What cheese does he recommend? (A wedge of Dorset, perhaps.) Those aren't the kinds of questions that generational farmers have traditionally been asked, and they may not be equipped to answer them. It's one of the (few) advantages second-career farmers have over generational farmers. There's an understanding of our urban customers, because we used to be one of them (or still are, in my case).

Cheese maker Margot Brooks has an interesting perspective on this question, since she has a foot in both worlds. A fifth-generation farmer, she was the first in her family to graduate from college, and she's been exposed to a much larger world, having lived in Europe.

Generational farmers, she says, sometimes have a jaundiced attitude toward things like farmers' markets. They are often

suspicious of the culture that lies outside their immediate farming community, the culture that has reduced people like them to
a country-bumpkin stereotype. Margot believes this isolationist
impulse started long before our time, when milk began to be
carted off to be pasteurized and homogenized, rather than sold on
the farm. That reduced the opportunities for farmers to interact
with consumers.

As Margot also points out, second-careerists like Rust and me
can outsource some of the more specialized farm chores that require the steepest learning curves—animal husbandry, for example. "Or you can get a fence guy to show you how to do rotational
grazing," she adds, referring to the technique of using fencing to
direct goats to fresh pasture. "But you can't teach an old farmer to
be social."

As a challenged newcomer to farming, I find it comforting to
add up the factors we might have in our favor: the mind-set we
share with our customers, sophisticated palates, outside
sources of income, a bevy of famous chefs and cookbook authors who give us moral support. But then a sobering thought
grips me: We still haven't managed to turn a profit, let alone get
rich farming. It makes you wonder what it takes.

AS WE WERE RAMPING UP ATTENDANCE AT FARMERS' MARKETS
in January, we were still trying to resolve the problem of our deal
with Polymeadows Farm. The issue had continued for months,

despite more than one attempt to suggest that the farm's owners, Melvin and Jennifer Lawrence, either reduce the goat milk supply they send or decrease their herd and produce less milk.

The whole arrangement was a miscalculation compounded by a misunderstanding. In July 2008, we had originally agreed that the Lawrences would supply the same amount of milk they had been selling to Vermont Butter & Cheese the previous year. And we agreed to use the same contract that they used with VB&C. However, the contract did not stipulate a cap on the milk supply quantity; at the time there was no reason to suspect that to be a bad thing. But then the family bought more goats and put them all out to pasture, so their production increased dramatically.

By December, we were at a tipping point, so on a Saturday afternoon shortly before Christmas, I had taken Melvin and Jennifer to the café at the Northshire Bookstore and reminded them that we were facing extremely precarious economic times. I showed them the projection numbers they had given us in July and what they had actually delivered, then asked them to keep to the original, lower numbers.

"It's going to be terrible," I said of the recession, "and if we can't pay for the milk, do you have a backup plan?"

Jennifer explained that their backup plan had been to make yogurt, but that we had strongly discouraged her from doing so. She was right about that. During that meeting in August, when I was so distracted by Mabelle and Rupee found wandering on the road, Jennifer had floated their idea to use our facility on weekends to make yogurt since she didn't have her own licensed facility, but we shot it down. Facing a crisis, we discussed it again then.

There had been and still were all sorts of questions and complications. Peter was afraid she might break or damage our equipment, or get hurt if unsupervised. So he wanted her working in the barn only if she hired one of our employees to oversee the operation. Rust wanted to know how much she was going to pay us, since he feared the operation would run up our electric bills. Jennifer would have to package her product at our place, so where was she going to store thousands of yogurt containers? What's more, Rust had done some research and didn't see how we would be able to sell the quantities she was contemplating making, nor how we'd be able to charge enough to turn a profit. Yogurt offers low profit potential. Rust did an informal survey and noticed that farmers' markets vendors rarely charged more than $2 a cup for yogurt. But Jennifer insisted that she could get $4 a cup.

After hashing through such matters again, the December meeting concluded with my giving Jennifer the green light on her yogurt project. But Melvin remained intractable about the milk supply.

The economy continued to deteriorate. Peter finally visited Polymeadows in January 2009 and told them the situation was unsustainable. They were producing eight hundred fifty pounds of milk a day, and we were lucky if we could use five hundred pounds. Our cheese vat didn't even hold that much milk. But Peter got nowhere with Melvin, who only said that he would rather quit than downsize. A week later, I was forced to send a termination letter, as required by our milk producer's agreement, giving them sixty days' notice.

I was sorry to have to do so, both for their sake and ours. Polymeadows has been in Melvin's family since the 1950s. They told me they'd have to sell the farm, though I recalled that before our arrangement, they'd somehow managed to survive selling lesser amounts to Vermont Butter & Cheese. Would this be the end of another Vermont farm? In the 1970s, there had been around two thousand family farms in the state; now we are down to about nine hundred.

I'm happy to say the farm managed to survive. Polymeadows Farm is now making yogurt and chèvre and selling their products at the Bennington Walloomsac Farmers' Market.

SEVERING OUR CONTRACT WITH POLYMEADOWS HAD PROFOUND practical implications for us. In 2008, our mind-set had been one of steady growth; the only question was whether we'd be able to produce enough cheese to satisfy demand. Sooner or later, by increasing production and cutting costs, we had been planning to turn a profit, hopefully by 2009. Our income in 2008, even with the downturn, was seven times what it had been in 2005. Our cheese-making capacity had soared, rising from twelve thousand pounds in 2006 to twenty-four thousand pounds in 2007, then doubling again to almost fifty thousand pounds in 2008.

This fissure and the financial crisis forced us to rethink our business model. Since the beginning of 2009, our plan has been to think smaller. This year we probably won't produce more than thirty-five thousand pounds of cheese. The milk will be sourced from our goats and Jersey Girls' cows, with a small additional amount of goat's milk coming from Noah's Arc Nubians. That's quite different from the one hundred thousand pounds of cheese we thought we might hit by 2009.

But even those smaller production numbers will require us to grow our herd if we're going to produce enough goat's milk on our own. Our new plan is to expand to eighty-five milking goats in 2010, up from forty-five in 2008. We had previously planned to keep few if any of this year's babies. Now we'll probably keep most or all of them. If we have thirty doelings this year and add them to the existing sixty-six we'll be milking in 2009, we should be able to raise our herd to close to one hundred head within a year or two. Honestly, I am thrilled to be able to keep more of our babies.

Fortunately, we have the space. Shortly before Christmas, we moved the milkers up to the old heifer barn. The farm's previous owners had milked dairy cows, so we first had to remove the cow-milking stanchions and clean out the barn. But the heifer barn presented several advantages over the lower barn. Because it's at a higher elevation, it's not as prone to flooding; the lower barn was vulnerable because it was built into a bank. The heifer barn is also easier to clean: The floor has a gutter where a mechanized chain cleaner carries away the old hay and goat waste, eliminating a lot of human labor. In the winter, that's not an issue, because we let the hay-pack pile up in order to provide the goats with a barrier and cushion against the barn's cold cement floor. But come spring, that apparatus will definitely make the barn easier to clean.

The move also frees up space in the lower barn, which will now be used exclusively for newborns and sick or injured goats, such as Natasha or Lailani, who can't keep up with the herd. When it comes time in March to separate the does from the bucks—who previously had the heifer barn all to themselves—hopefully the weather will cooperate and we'll be able to have the does outdoors browsing on pasture day and night, with the bucks confined to the barn and to a small, fenced-in corral behind it.

Where the bucks are kept may not make a difference for Boris. Previously, I wasn't worried about a little in-family breeding in the herd because I was planning to sell or give away this year's doelings. Now that I'm keeping them, I'll also need to replenish the gene pool. That means new bucks. Tyrone will still have a job, because he hasn't sired any of the does with whom he'll breed next fall. However, I'll have to find a new home for Boris. He'll probably stay with us until October, when goat farmers suddenly realize they need a buck for breeding—and they'll need Boris's expertise at wooing the women.

I'm relieved that I'll no longer have to worry about paying huge milk bills. And I'm hopeful we'll still find a way to turn a profit, even when making less cheese—by reining in costs, keeping the staff as lean as possible, and increasing sales.

The recession of 2008 was just one more example of learning to roll with the punches. After all was said and done, we could take solace in a few things: knowing that the cheese we made was now consistently great; that we were manufacturing a wide-enough variety of cheeses to appeal to most tastes; that we had a first-rate team; and that we were learning through necessity to watch and cut expenses carefully. If and when our fortunes turned, we would be poised to take advantage of it. And that's what happened in February.

SIXTEEN

accolades and accusations

FRESH POSITIVE SIGNS CAME IN EARLY FEBRUARY DURING A media luncheon held at the Boathouse Restaurant in New York's Central Park. The event was sponsored by the Vermont Department of Tourism & Marketing to showcase the state's bounty— not the easiest feat in the dead of winter, when our fields were lying under a foot of heavy snow. Nevertheless, a delicious meal was whipped up by Amy Chamberlain, owner-chef of The Perfect Wife, a restaurant in Manchester, Vermont. It started with her cheddar-ale soup, a velvety concoction made with Vermont Grafton Village Cheddar and Long Trail Ale. Next it moved on to Amy's lovely turkey schnitzel, then finally the desserts: maple panna cotta, apple-walnut turnover, and warm chocolate cake. Capping it off were three of our award-winning cheeses: Manchester, Pawlet, and Dorset.

Regis Philbin, veteran host of *Live with Regis and Kelly*, fell in love with our cheese. Sitting at a nearby table with Vermont Governor Jim Douglas, he so enjoyed the cheese that I was called over to tell him about it. He even called me "sweetie," which no one, including my husband, has called me for ages. (In Rust's defense, he did send me a Valentine's card this year—a first. It had a picture of a sheep and the sentiment, "I'm mad about ewe." Inside he noted, "I couldn't find a goat.")

On *Live* shortly after, Regis discussed the luncheon with Kelly Ripa during the host-chat segment. While she took repeated nips from a little bottle of maple syrup that had been included in everybody's goodie bag, he sang the praises of Vermont cheese. Though, unfortunately, not ours. The piece of cheese he handed Kelly to sample was Cabot Cheddar. We were crushed. But as they say, that's show business. Though we missed our fifteen minutes of fame on *Live*, Consider Bardwell Farm did get a mention in a nice write-up of the event in the *Rutland Herald*, Vermont's second largest daily. We welcomed it, even though the newspaper, fine as it is, doesn't have quite the same ripple effect as a nationally syndicated TV show.

But being showcased at the Vermont Department of Tourism & Marketing event was just one sign that our luck was changing. We were learning how to scramble, to seize marketing opportunities where they existed, and to create them where they didn't. Throughout

February, we continued to focus on adding sales outlets. To supplement the growing but inconsistent sales from farmers' markets, we made a deal with Provisions in which Consider Bardwell would be the featured cheese maker for a network of twenty-five Vermont food co-ops. As part of the deal, we agreed to sell them our Manchester and Dorset at a discount and they would chop their own profit margins. We decided to take the hit because it would raise awareness of the farm and help sell our oversupply of cheese.

And just when we thought the economy was dead, both Jasper Hill and Provisions surprised us with large cheese orders, and we were on something of a roll with free publicity. The week before their Vermont luncheon feature, the *Rutland Herald* also ran a piece about the debut of our Equinox cheese at the Equinox Spa and Resort in Manchester, Vermont, one of the state's most luxurious resorts. Chris connected the cheese to the nearby Equinox Mountain. "It's a mountainous, big, bold cheese," he said, waxing poetic about our aged, hard goat's cheese.

According to Equinox's head chef, Jeffrey Russell, it also grates quite well. "We tried it last night over pasta," Russell told the *Rutland Herald*. "It has a nice little spark to it." Equinox would become the official grated cheese of their tavern's lobster spaghetti.

Though not a feature story in *The New York Times*, the *Rutland Herald* article was good for morale. Peter had spent a couple of months tinkering with the Equinox recipe to get it right.

Then in early March, a piece on the *Chicago Sun-Times*'s website listed Manchester on their Top 10 list of "stink-a-licious" cheeses—a good thing for fans of assertive cheeses.

We all needed the lift to keep us going but couldn't get too comfortable because we were hit by another unexpected crisis: the threat of a diseased herd.

The alarm came in an email from a Vermont farmer who bought three of our doelings the preceding month. He said that he had found bumps or abscesses on all three and that they likely had CL, or caseous lymphadenitis. Also called pseudotuberculosis, this is a serious contagious disease that can spread to other animals in the herd when the abscesses burst. It can even lead to death. It's considered the curse of the goat industry throughout the world.

When the man had originally called, he told me he was starting up a herd and was looking for Oberhaslis. Before he came for the goats in January, I'd made a special effort to select and sell him only those with pedigrees that I could vouch for. We had one baby who had lost her identity necklace, which meant that her pedigree—the identities of her mother and father—were lost to the ages. We named her Jane Doe. For that reason, I wouldn't have sold her to him.

I wasn't at the farm when he came to pick up the goats. Alex Eaton handled the transaction and told me that he seemed serious and knowledgeable. That made his accusations all the more disturbing.

His email said: "I would hate to think you knowingly culled and sold me CL-positive animals, but three for three is pretty damning. CL must be rampant in your herd. I can't imagine that it has escaped your notice."

I was dumbfounded. We keep careful watch over our animals and were fairly confident that CL was not even present, let alone rampant, in the herd. Months earlier, when two older milkers, Magnolia and Zoe, were discovered to have lumps, we had them officially tested immediately, and they came out negative for CL.

Nevertheless, the farmer's email spurred us into action. In February, we inspected every goat from that group: the babies born in 2008, who were now almost a year old. They were all healthy. Not a single one had a lump or any other telltale sign.

I called the farmer at home as soon as I got his emails. I left a message on his voicemail and emailed several times, explaining that two milkers had neck abscesses the previous summer, but were tested and cleared for CL. In any case, neither had ever been in contact with the kids. I suggested that he have the doelings tested, or alternatively, I offered to come and get the goats and return his $255. Out of concern for both our herds, I also wanted more details: Did they just have lumps, or were they abscesses that came to the surface and burst?

But he never returned my call. I don't know if it was a false alarm and the tests came back negative. My fear is that he never tested at all and simply destroyed the animals.

THIS INCIDENT WAS A REALLY UPSETTING DISTRACTION, BUT we kept working on finding new ways to generate income. We decided to hold monthly cheese-making workshops led by Peter.

Our first, scheduled for early March, targeted farmers rather than urban second-careerists. The $350 workshop fee included a two-day course, breakfasts and lunches, and an overnight stay. I set up four bedrooms in the main house and three in the rental house across the road, which had been gussied up for new renters who were moving in on April 1.

Nine people signed up. Our first arrival, a lovely woman who had acquired two of my favorite goats a couple of years earlier, nonetheless convinced me that I was not cut out for the hospitality industry. She decided she could not stay in the newly painted house across the street because she was allergic to chemical fumes. So I switched her to the main house, moving another of the workshop participants across the street. Then she explained that she'd brought her own food because she has type O blood, and, according to a book she was following, *Eat Right for Your Type*, she shouldn't consume any gluten and wheat.

I'm from the school of "Eat everything on your plate, and don't even wrinkle your nose." But today, many people have very special nutrition requirements. I know my limitations, and dealing with "hold the pickles, hold the lettuce" people is one of them.

We expected the workshop to generate about $3,500. Peter would take $1,000, and the farm would get the rest. It's not a huge amount of money, but it helps.

The teaching was on Peter's shoulders. I was the behind-the-scenes stage manager. Moving out of the house to free up my bedroom for guests was a burden for me, but probably even more so for my gracious friend Pippa. (Pippa's house is where I usually head as a retreat from my own.) I also had to feed everybody, make them comfortable, and wash all the sheets and towels, both before and after the event. The $2,500 earnings wound up evaporating almost instantly to pay for hay, grain, wood shavings, and powdered milk for the babies, but from this trial run we realized that workshops are a viable enterprise and good for our balance sheet.

Rust and I are excited about the workshops because they add a whole other dimension to the farm as a destination. We're doing one a month. We get to meet new people. I get to interact with other farmers, and we share ideas. When they leave, they buy a ton of cheese. We had a man from Florida who bought $50 worth of cheese after the workshop, then came back for the Vermont Cheese Festival in August and bought another $900 of cheese to be shipped to him. Peter is pleased with the arrangement, too. He used to travel all over the country and the world teaching people how to make cheese. Now he doesn't have to leave Vermont as often. His students can travel to him.

BY NOW, SPRING WAS JUST AROUND THE CORNER, AND THIS year I finally got to enjoy that transitional time, having remained at the farm for a solid week prior to the workshop in order to prep the house and farm. During that respite from my agenting work, I wrote. Taking advantage of the peace and quiet, I'd sit at my computer typing and gazing out the bedroom window, which looked directly onto the spring-fed pond that fueled the water-wheel my predecessor Consider Bardwell built so many years ago. The days were getting noticeably longer, and once again promise was in the air. The geese were getting ready to lay eggs, and the ganders were attentive, protective, and a bit possessive. Soon the geese would be sitting on nests filled with giant eggs, each the equivalent of three large chicken eggs. I've seen up to twenty eggs in a clutch in years past and have occasionally stolen one or two to make my Gosling Lemon Pound Cake, which was always a hit at the West Pawlet Fish and Game Café and regularly shows up on our traditional Easter lunch menu.

I watched our three Pekin ducks swimming together, dunking their heads and shoulders under the water and kicking their orange legs and feet up in the air. It looked like fun. This trio is new. For months, we had only one lonely Pekin. Part of a pair, he had escaped a predator's attack, but his mate had been taken out. Since then, the little duck had been trailing after our three snow geese, trying to be part of their group. He somehow managed to survive the pecking they assaulted him with every morning when he tried to compete for the corn and bread crumbs we scattered.

Rust had been trying to find a mate for the duck. It was difficult this time of year, because sources like Tractor Supply and Agway don't start selling baby fowl until later in the spring.

Serendipitously, the Sunday before the workshop, someone knocked on our kitchen door and asked if he could leave his two Pekin ducks on our pond. I couldn't believe it. As he explained, he and his wife own an inn in Manchester and a predator had killed their other two Pekins. To protect the survivors, they'd kept the duo in a barn all winter long. The man said they were languishing for want of swimming and washing, because ducks like to be clean. When Rust walked into the kitchen, I exclaimed that a small miracle had just happened: Our Pekin would have companions.

Later that afternoon, the man, whose name I never learned, brought the two over in a dog kennel and gently nudged them into the water. Our little duck swam right over to them and off the three sailed. I call them Nina, Pinta, and Santa Maria. It turns out that our duck is a real Nina, but the other two are guys. Since it seems they're fighting over her affections, perhaps we'll have some ducklings come May, along with a gaggle of goslings and about one hundred baby goats.

SEVENTEEN

endings and beginnings

DESPITE MY SENTIMENTAL CONNECTION TO SOME OF THE goats, even I have had to acknowledge when it was time to let go. We were forced to euthanize Lailani, one of my favorites, on June 1. Lailani, who was only five years old (goats can remain productive milkers until they're ten or twelve and live to be fifteen), couldn't even stand up to graze and had become emaciated. She'd had two baby boys this 2009 kidding season, and we allowed her to tend to them until the day they left us to be fattened up on Sara Cohen's farm. They learned to nurse while their mother was lying down, an unusual nursing position. They gave Lailani something to live for. But come weaning time, they had to go with the other little bucklings, and Lailani had to be moved out of the milkers' area.

After they departed, we transferred her to the yearling field across the street, where she spent most of her time lying down and crying out. I knew that this was no way for her to live. I called the vet and asked her to come to put her down.

I alerted Bob Hahn to get ready for a funeral. When we are forced to euthanize one of the goats, it's Bob who loads her onto a tractor and carts her away to be buried. He takes the job seriously and solemnly. When Petunia died in April, Bob even planted petunias on her grave.

When the vet arrived, Lailani was lying on the far end of the pasture. But wouldn't you know it, as soon as she saw the vet, she stood up and started to walk in the opposite direction. I'd never seen her trot so majestically even though her back legs were bent in half and she couldn't stand on her feet. She hadn't been able to walk properly for over eighteen months, and standing was very painful for her. I took her gently by the collar and held her head while the vet inserted a syringe into her jugular vein. Lailani was perfectly docile. She simply fell sideways while I was still holding her and stroking her face. The whole thing took less than a minute. None of the staff could bear to be there for her last moments, but we had all agreed—as did the vet—that this sad occasion was long overdue. Lailani was a hero to have been able to bear those last two little baby boys, who will produce income for the farm. She worked till the end.

I thought I'd be a basket case, but I wasn't. I knew that I did the right thing, that Lailani would no longer be miserable. I even tried to lighten the mood after it was over, telling Bob he needed to buy a trumpet to play "Taps."

🐐

DESPITE ITS TRAGEDIES, THE GLORY OF A FARM IS THAT IT IS truly a celebration of life. Whether you're raising goats and making cheese or growing vegetables, it's primarily about birth and growth and productivity.

In Vermont, spring begins more or less when the temperature creeps above freezing for the first time in months, usually around the beginning of April.

One day, Alex Eaton tried to lead Tallulah, a half brown–half black yearling due to give birth shortly, up the ramp to the milking parlor, while Minny stood at the top of the ramp trying to coax the animal from there. It was probably Tallulah's tenth training session in the milking room.

Milkers aren't born knowing how to behave on a production line; they have to be taught by repeating the drill every day for several weeks before they kid and then giving them a tasty reward: grain pellets that you deposit in a trough right under their noses.

But this season's rookies, born, like Tallulah, in 2007, have proved more problematic and less cooperative than those from previous years. The reason is simple: They are the class we let stay on their mothers for eight weeks after they were born. As Alex pointed out, they associate their mothers, rather than humans, with food. He calls them "antisocial"—with people, of course. They're perfectly in sync with their herd.

The group from 2008, now eleven months old, are just the opposite. Because we separated them at birth, they've bonded to us rather than to their mothers. "They love us," Alex observed. "You walk in their pen, and they swarm. They're a much more friendly bunch than the yearlings. You walk into the yearling pen, and they scatter."

Nonetheless, the yearlings are slowly getting with the program. They should be fully trained by the time they start delivering their babies in a couple of weeks, even if some kinks remain to be worked out. For example, they obediently follow orders until it's time to insert their heads into the milking stanchions. The stanchions are supposed to secure them in place, spacing them out evenly and making it possible to milk them. But some stick their heads into the space *between* the stanchions. Those with horns can get stuck in the empty spaces and need help getting extracted, which makes the process even more challenging and time-consuming.

But they're reluctantly coming around to the realization that there is a routine to follow. The first day Alex and Minny put them through their paces, Alex recalled indelicately that "half of them crapped" in the milking parlor and were shaking from the trauma. Now only one, Orchid, continues to have problems. She's clearly her mother's daughter, born of Lailani two years ago. "She's just as much an outcast as her mother was," Alex said. "She's very reclusive and disliked by everybody"—by goats and, on occasion, humans, too.

Natasha, whom we were worried about, seems to be doing OK, even though she's had some troubles. The daughter of Nadia and sister of Boris, Natasha was the one milker who remained unbred in 2008. She'd been sick on and off all summer with some problem that had eluded diagnosis. It started when we noticed her taking her weight off one leg and lagging behind the other goats. Dr. Alderink, our vet, determined that it was a shoulder problem. We thought it might have become hyperextended when she was feeding and trying to reach for some hay.

We put Natasha on antibiotics, which meant we couldn't milk her. We also separated her from the rest of the herd, placing her in sick bay, a pen set aside for special cases, since goats can be merciless when one of their own displays weakness or infirmity. And they already had, shoving her out of the way to get to the hay or grain, which risked aggravating her injury.

Natasha, who is four years old, didn't seem to mind being alone, which is unusual for goats, who are herd animals. But she also didn't seem to be getting any better. When she couldn't even get to her feet one day, I called Dr. Alderink and told her I thought I had another goat that needed to be euthanized. The vet clearly didn't believe that, because when she came over, she unceremoniously grabbed Natasha by her collar and lifted her to her feet. It turned out that the goat hadn't been able to get up because she had been lying on her injured shoulder. Possibly the shoulder had gone to sleep, and she equated the sensation with pain and stopped moving.

She soon started walking sideways, and Minny nicknamed her "Neck" because she seemed unable to straighten it out. "People are going to think you're doing experiments on her," our sarcastic Minny said.

Natasha remains what Alex calls a "crazy nightmare," an enduring maintenance challenge. She can't see where she's going as she runs around, and she often trips and falls. Natasha is now living with the yearlings across the street. And we finally discovered what was wrong with her: A meningeal worm attacked her spinal column, paralyzing her neck, but she's still alive and functioning.

GETTING THE YEARLINGS USED TO THE MILKING PARLOR was only one of the preparations for spring. We also had to make sure they received their vaccinations: one for tetanus, the other a parasiticide, or dewormer, used to control things like roundworms, lungworms, grubs, and so on. Alex, who is bright and cheerful and increasingly indispensable to the barn's operation, was in charge of that. He and Minny also trimmed the babies' hooves and would spend a full day cleaning out the baby pen as we prepared to turn the barn into a maternity ward.

Our midwife, Laura Fletcher, arrived on March 20. We had been in frequent touch as she double-checked to make sure we had all the supplies for her arrival (and the babies'): iodine to disinfect umbilical chords, a stethoscope to listen to heartbeats and lung wheezes, and squeeze bulbs to suction mucus out of the newborns' nose and throat as soon as they emerge from their mother's womb.

Alex and Minny's mountain of chores served as a test of how well they worked as a team, and I was relieved to see they passed with flying colors. Their relationship didn't start auspiciously last summer, when Alex was new to the farm. Minny feared he was muscling in on her responsibilities and would eventually supplant her. She needn't have worried. Since Leslie introduced Minny, her best friend, to the farm a year ago, my respect and affection for her have steadily grown, even if her strident, conservative views occasionally rankle. She's responsible, hardworking, insightful, and very funny. Her undiluted cynicism (unusual for someone her age) and more than occasional foul mouth just add to her nineteen-year-old charm.

She also seems to have developed grudging respect for Alex, realizing that he's not a "loser" just because Margot and he go for walks, read at night, and don't own a TV.

Politics continues to be a source of usually good-natured friction on the farm. Our staff now finally seem to be able to see past the caricatures they'd had of each other: Margot and Alex of Minny as a gun-toting, pickup-driving redneck; Minny of Margot as a bleeding-heart liberal. (However, the bumper stickers on Margot's Toyota—"Love Your Mother" with a picture of the Earth; "Keep Your Butts in the Car: The Earth Is Not Your Ashtray"—continue to spark mischievous fantasies of vandalism on Minny's part.)

Alex believes that Minny no longer sees him as a threat to her livelihood, and he doesn't dismiss her as some sort of potty-mouthed hick.

Meanwhile, Margot's relationship with Leslie, with whom she

is alone for hours every week in the cheese room, is flourishing. Leslie has always attached herself to older female mentors such as Debbie Tracy, and Margot believes that Leslie regards her as something of a big sister.

Margot and Alex have become integral to making the farm run smoothly. It's a great relief having them living in the smithy and knowing that they care deeply and put in the effort to learn how everything works. They're hungry for the knowledge they might use one day to start cheese making with Margot's family.

Margot's positive attitude also has something to do with the knowledge that Polymeadows is out of the picture and with it the tsunami of milk they were sending. She confessed that she's a lot less anxious about the summer. Last summer, she was working sixty-hour weeks. This summer, she's looking forward to forty- to forty-five-hour weeks and lots of vegetable gardening.

Leslie, who had been difficult in the past, questioning my decisions and dismissing me as a dilettante, is working hard to develop more of an adult relationship with me. She spent a lot of time helping out during our cheese-making workshop and even complimented my cooking. She's willing to try new dishes, like the Middle Eastern roasted-eggplant spread that she would have rejected not too long ago as suspiciously foreign. As a matter of fact, she turned to Minny during one of the April cheese-making workshop meals and chided her for not knowing what it was. "It's *baba ganoush!*" she declared.

She even offered me animal husbandry advice one day. "Why don't you buy a French Alpine and breed it with the Oberhasli?"

she suggested. "You'll get better milk." That was a bit more than Minny could take. Looking down her nose at Leslie (as only Minny can), she reminded her best friend, "You work in the cheese room now."

We recently held a cheese tasting for this season's first batch of Manchester. We had to tinker with the recipe since we're now using only our own milk and no longer buying any from Poly-meadows Farm. That means the fat and protein content in the milk is different than it used to be. When Leslie tried it, Rust, who'd once dismissed her as a moody teenager, was absolutely astonished by the subtlety of her palate and her ability to trans-late her tasting experiences into words. (Fortunately, the cheese was great!)

I also couldn't be more proud of Chris. As challenging as the economic environment is, he has kept the cash coming in. He's still itching to be as involved as possible with the farm and the cheese-making operation. But I'm convinced that his success in drumming up business has a lot to do with staying in New York, working the phones, and making calls on customers.

In the first two months of 2009 alone, we took in about $55,000. That sounds great, but we had only $450 of that left in our checking account after I paid all the bills. But at least we had something left over.

Winter into early spring is the time of year when we have the fewest expenses. The goats don't cost anything because they're liv-ing off the hay we stockpiled last summer. We're not feeding them grain, except for the treats we give to persuade them to visit the milking parlor; otherwise, they're just lazing around the barn waiting to have their babies, and they don't need the extra protein. There are also few, if any, vet bills, because we are always monitoring the goats and tending to their needs.

The low flow of activity and bills will change shortly and dramatically, of course, when they start kidding, and my money worries will begin again. I'll have to buy grain for the lactating mothers. We'll have to feed the babies when we pull them off their mothers—which, based on our experience last year and in consultation with the vet, will be when they are three days old. That will mean purchasing $1,500 worth of Save-A-Kid, the expensive powdered goat milk, which can cost up to $75 for a twenty-five-pound bag, unless you go deal hunting. We do a lot of shopping around before settling on a supplier.

MY RELATIONSHIP WITH RUST COULDN'T BE BETTER. THE only problem, from the point of view of the farm, which he has really taken to, is that his architectural practice continues to flourish. He wavers between being really happy (and relieved, given the economy) and worried that his obligations on the farm will distract him from paying clients who might fire him because the architectural drawings aren't completed on time. For the sake of his business, he really ought to spend a solid two months in the city and not be commuting up to the farm. As it is, these days he spends weekends up here, returns with me to the city on Monday afternoon or Tuesday morning, checks in on his city projects, then heads out to Shelter Island to tend to clients there on Wednesday or Thursday.

Luckily he can help even from a distance. That became apparent once again during the first morning of the April cheese-making workshop, when Margot slipped into the house as everyone was having breakfast and whispered that there was no heat or hot water in the barn. Twelve people—including a father and daughter from Shanghai and someone who had flown in from Florida—had paid to make cheese, and the machinery was turning on us. Margot had been readying the cheese vat, but there would be no cheese, and no workshop, if we couldn't heat the milk.

I left the house as unobtrusively as possible and went to the barn. I had to make believe I knew what I was doing, if only to calm down Margot and Leslie. I'm a lot more confident about running the farm than I was even a year ago. I can look at the goats and pretty accurately diagnose their health problems. This spring marks the sixth time we'll have gone through the annual cycle of kidding, milking, cheese making, breeding, and drying them off for the winter, and I've internalized the process by now. It doesn't seem nearly as scary as it used to, even though the onset of kidding—anticipating the unexpected—still intimidates me.

But there are still things over my head, and one of them is misbehaving machinery. I checked the boiler. I could tell it was on, but for some reason it wouldn't fire up. I called Rust in New York, put him on the speakerphone, and had him walk me through every pipe and valve until he finally found the valve that had been turned off.

Actually, the problem was his fault. He had done it on Tuesday before he left for the city, because the pressure of the water running into the hot-water tank had been too high. In order to lower it, he switched the valve off but forgot to turn it back on.

If I hadn't been able to get in touch with him—if he'd been in a meeting with a client, for example—the first day of the workshop could have been a catastrophe. But since we got the problem fixed and the workshop participants were none the wiser about the drama unfolding while they ate their yogurt and fruit, coffee, and pure raw milk, the workshop proved a success.

LAST YEAR, I USED TO DAYDREAM ABOUT RENTING OUT THE farm for weddings, but decided that I don't need the headache. Does that suggest I'm changing? That I'm not necessarily biologically programmed to take on too much? Am I getting old and lazy, or finally growing up? Have I put the ghosts of my mother's failed ambitions behind me, as well as the belief that I have to do ten things at once to rationalize my existence? Perhaps. I can now see that there's a sweet spot between anxiety-filled insomnia on the one hand, and guilt-ridden indolence on the other. Getting other people to do the heavy lifting isn't a sign of weakness, but of good management skills. As a matter of fact, I'm looking forward to spending more time than ever in the city during kidding season, knowing the farm will be in safe hands, between Laura, Alex, Margot, Chris, Minny, Leslie, and Peter.

Fortunately, my agenting business keeps chugging along. I do often rush back to the city to have lunches with authors and negotiate contracts with editors when I'm not preoccupied with goats. Although six-figure advances aren't a thing of the past, they are far less common than they were just a couple of years ago—but we're still making deals. It's enough to help support us.

If I had to do it all over again, would I have been content to do nothing with the farm other than entertain weekend guests and work on the Sunday *New York Times* crossword? Of course not.

Samantha pointed out that I always seem to need a project. What more glorious project than this? There's so much beauty here, plus there is the privilege of getting to learn about goats and provide for their welfare, the opportunity to create a clean, healthy food product that adds a little something extra to people's lives using environmentally sound practices, and the pride of doing so alongside coworkers from different walks of life who have come together for a common purpose.

On that day in March when Alex was training the goats to be milkers, it was muddy as only Vermont can be and overcast, but warm. Spring was definitely in the air. You could feel the earth awakening. You could smell it as the ground started to thaw. And the goats felt it, too. They were much more active than they'd been even a few days earlier, venturing further out into the pasture behind the barn and behaving like kids: Mothers with swollen bellies, only days away from giving birth, were running sideways and kicking up their heels.

THE FIFTH ANNIVERSARY OF OUR BEING A LICENSED creamery came on July 2, 2009, which also happened to be Samantha's birthday. Just to get certified in 2004 cost us hundreds of thousands of dollars in equipment and construction. We've spent hundreds of thousands more since then. But everything seems in place for us to succeed—if perhaps a little slower than I would have liked.

I remain convinced, along with my team, that we're going to make it. On some days, that belief may be fueled by nothing more tangible than the sight of the goats grazing industriously in the pasture behind the barn, their babies playing in the kindergarten enclosure, the blades on the cheese vat whirring as milk turns to Manchester, and hundreds of wheels aging in the cheese caves, readying for market. Or we might be at full throttle, kidding, milking, and cheese making. All are reason to celebrate.

RECIPES

THE BARDWELL CHEESE COURSE
Makes 4 servings

Cheese lovers know that eating cheese—particularly artisanal cheese—right out of the wrapping may be the most pleasurable way to enjoy it. However, to take the next step and offer a selection of cheeses in a range of styles, try the following six Consider Bardwell Farm cheeses. I've described each cheese's style to help you make substitutions.

The cheeses will speak for themselves without any additions, but feel free to serve them with accompaniments such as quince paste, honey, savory jams, nuts, or fruits, which enhance and balance the flavors of the cheeses.

2 Mettowee crottins of chèvre

¼ pound Rupert—Alpine cow's milk cheese, aged one year as a 30-pound wheel

¼ pound Pawlet—Italian-style toma, aged 6 months as a 10-pound wheel

¼ pound Manchester—washed-rind goat's milk tomme, aged 3–4 months as a 3-pound wheel

¼ pound Dorset—washed-rind cow's milk cheese, aged 2–4 months as a 3-pound wheel

¼ pound Equinox—a hard, extra-aged, raw goat's milk cheese inspired by Italian sardos like Piave and Asiago

1. Set out four dessert-sized plates.
2. Cut the chèvre into eight slices, two for each plate.
3. Cut each of the remaining cheeses, in the order listed above, into flat triangles and arrange two to each plate.
4. The cheeses can be best enjoyed when moving from the mildest, the chèvre, to the strongest, the Equinox.

SPICY FRESH QUESO BLANCO

WHITE CHEESE

Makes approximately one 8-ounce cup

My first attempt at making cheese at home was this simple Mexican-style *queso blanco*, which is similar in texture to farmers' cheese. I leave the more sophisticated cheeses to our professional cheese makers and still make this one on my own.

There are no tricks to making this cheese. All you do is bring the milk just to its boiling point, then add acid in the form of vinegar or citrus juice. Use a thermometer to make sure the milk reaches the correct temperature.

You can flavor the cheese in innumerable ways. I like to give it some kick with chiles or dried red pepper flakes, which I always seem to have in the house, and sun-dried tomatoes for richness.

The mild, soft cheese absorbs flavor easily while marinating and becomes delicious.

Serve crumbled on salad greens—just add vinegar or a light, tart dressing.

2 quarts raw goat's milk (or any milk, including store-bought cow's milk)

¼ cup acid (white vinegar or citrus juice such as lemon or lime)

Salt to taste

1 cup olive oil

2 tablespoons slivered sun-dried tomatoes

1 tablespoon seeded, chopped jalapeños or red pepper flakes (optional)

1. In a medium pot, heat the milk over medium heat to just below boiling—about 185°F. Remove from the heat and add the acid slowly, stirring constantly. The curds and whey will start to separate right away.

2. Line a strainer or colander with cheesecloth. When the curds

261

are fully separated, remove them with a slotted spoon and place them in the strainer.

3. Tie the ends of the cheesecloth together and hang it to drain over the sink faucet for at least two hours or overnight. (You can also tie the cheesecloth around a heavy wooden spoon, then hang the spoon over the edges of a pot to allow the cheese to drain into the pot.) Make sure that it is no longer dripping whey.

4. When the cheese is dry, cut it into cubes.

5. Put the cheese into a small bowl, sprinkle with salt, and toss to coat. Add the olive oil, sun-dried tomatoes, and jalapeño or red pepper flakes and let marinate in the refrigerator for at least two hours. Cheese will keep (in the refrigerator in a covered container) about four days.

WATERMELON AND TOMATO SALAD
Makes 4 servings

Thanks to Mark Bittman and his new edition of *How to Cook Everything*, I have fallen in love with the combination of watermelon and juicy August tomatoes from my vegetable garden. I garnish the combination with our feta-style cheese, which we call Danby. Most feta is made from sheep's milk, but ours has the tang of our goat's milk. Briny Danby obviates the need to salt this cool combo. This recipe offers a beautiful presentation, but feel free to cut up the fruits into chunks and toss them together with the cheese.

> *4 medium heirloom tomatoes, thickly sliced*
>
> *¼ watermelon, seeded, peeled, and cut into slices of similar thickness to the*
>   *tomatoes*
>
> *4 ounces Danby or any feta cheese, crumbled*
>
> *Extra virgin olive oil to drizzle*
>
> *Pepper to taste*

1. Set out four salad plates. On each plate, stack the slices of one tomato, alternating with the watermelon slices.
2. Sprinkle the Danby over each stack, drizzle with olive oil, and add pepper to taste. Serve at room temperature.

MUSHROOM BREAD PUDDING
Makes 8 servings

Before I became the literary agent of chef-restaurateur Jean-Georges Vongerichten, I was a fan of his food, particularly this bread pudding, which I discovered in an article in *The New York Times* many years ago. I still make it, but now I have my own variations. In this version, I use two Consider Bardwell Farm cheeses, which transform this dish into a silky, sublime main course. A tartly dressed salad is a perfect accompaniment. I also like to serve it as a side dish at parties.

2 tablespoons unsalted butter, plus more for greasing the pan

1 cup grated (about 4 ounces) of any Alpine cheese (I use Consider Bardwell Farm one-year-old Rupert)

8 ounces crusty baguette, cut into 1-inch cubes

½ cup grated (about 2 ounces) hard cheese, such as Parmigiano Reggiano or Pecorino Romano (I use Consider Bardwell Farm Equinox goat's milk cheese)

4 ounces mixed fresh wild mushrooms, such as shiitake, enoki, chanterelles, and oysters, thinly sliced

2 leeks, thinly sliced and well rinsed

¹/₃ cup chard stems, diced

3 cups chopped chard leaves

1 large egg

¾ cup whole milk

¾ cup heavy cream

Salt and freshly ground black pepper

1. Preheat the oven to 400°F. Use a little of the butter to grease the inside of a 2-quart casserole (or 8 x 8-inch baking dish). Set aside ¼ cup of the Alpine cheese. Mix the bread and remaining Alpine and grating cheese in a large bowl.

2. In a large skillet over medium-low heat, melt 1 tablespoon butter, then sauté the mushrooms, leeks, and chard stems for about 5 minutes, stirring to coat vegetables evenly; cook until softened. Add the vegetable mixture to the bowl containing the bread and cheeses.

3. Add the remaining butter to the skillet. Sauté the chard leaves until wilted, then transfer them to the mixing bowl.

4. In a medium bowl, beat the egg until blended.

5. In a small saucepan, combine the milk and heavy cream and bring to a boil over medium-low heat. Remove from the heat, and pour about 1 cup of the hot milk mixture into the egg, whisking constantly. Then pour the egg and milk mixture back into the saucepan, whisking until blended and heated through.

6. Pour the egg and milk mixture over the dry ingredients and stir together. Season with salt and pepper, and transfer the mixture to the baking pan. Bake for about 25 minutes. Remove the pan from the oven when you've tested the mixture with a fork and it comes out dry or just barely moist.

7. Preheat the broiler. Unmold the pudding onto a flat broiler-proof pan. Sprinkle the reserved Alpine cheese on top and place under the broiler until golden brown, about 3 to 4 minutes. Serve hot.

TOMATO TART WITH RUPERT AND HERBS

Makes one 9-inch tart (plus an extra pie crust)

When I had the Fish and Game Café in West Pawlet, I worked hard to perfect tart making, both savory and sweet. One that I particularly loved and that was popular at the café was inspired by *Once Upon a Tart*, a cookbook by Frank Mentesana and Jerome Audureau with Carolynn Carreño (Knopf). I was not the agent for the book, but the buzz about it led me to try its recipes. My adaptation is simpler (I'm hardly a professional baker) and features Consider Bardwell's Rupert, a nutty and robust Alpine cheese. The book's recipe for Provençal Tart calls for Gruyère. The Rupert can certainly be replaced with Gruyère, Emmentaler, or any standard Swiss cheese, but it won't be as good!

You only use one crust for the tart, but this simple recipe makes two 9-inch crusts. (Save the second for later use. It can be frozen, covered securely in plastic wrap, for up to one month.)

THE CRUST

2½ cups unbleached all-purpose flour

3 tablespoons semolina flour

1 teaspoon salt

12 tablespoons (1½ sticks) cold unsalted butter, cut into ¼-inch cubes

3 tablespoons cold solid vegetable shortening

Glass of ice water

THE FILLING

12 plum tomatoes, cored and cut into ¼-inch rounds

2 tablespoons Dijon mustard

1 cup coarsely grated Rupert (or other Alpine-style) cheese

½ teaspoon chopped fresh rosemary

½ teaspoon chopped fresh thyme

266

2 large eggs

¼ cup light cream

Salt and pepper to taste

1. Make the crust: Preheat the oven to 400°F.

2. In the bowl of a food processor fitted with a metal blade, combine the two flours and salt using only two or three pulses. Add the butter and shortening and pulse about 10 to 15 times, until the mixture forms moist crumbs. (No visible butter or shortening bits should remain.)

3. Remove the dough crumbs from the food processor and put them into a large bowl. Sprinkle 4 tablespoons of ice water over the surface of the dough. Using your hands, work the dough into a ball. Add more water if needed, but don't let the dough become wet. Cut the ball in half and wrap each half in plastic. Flatten each into a disk and refrigerate for at least 30 minutes or overnight.

4. Roll out one disk to ¼ inch thick. Fit it into the tart pan and chill for another 30 minutes. Then prick the bottom of the tart shell with a fork. Cover the dough with aluminum foil and cover the foil with pie weights or dried beans.

5. Bake the tart shell for 10 minutes. Remove the pie weights and foil, and set the shell aside to cool.

6. Make the filling: Position the oven rack in the center of the oven. Reduce the oven to 375°F. Drain the tomatoes in a strainer or colander for about 30 minutes.

7. Spread the mustard evenly over the bottom of the tart shell. Sprinkle the cheese and herbs over the mustard. Lay the

drained tomato slices in overlapping concentric circles on top of the cheese layer, working from the inside out and covering the entire crust.

8. Whisk the eggs in a small bowl and whisk in the light cream, salt, and pepper. Pour the custard over the tomatoes to about ¼ inch from the top edge of the crust. (If you don't have enough, stir a little more light cream into the custard.)

9. Bake the tart for about 1 hour and 20 minutes, or until the custard has set in the center. (The tomatoes will give off a pinkish liquid that should not be confused with uncooked eggs. The liquid will evaporate as the tart cools.)

10. Transfer the tart from the oven to a wire rack and let it cool slightly. To remove the tart from the pan, gently set it on a large can, and the outside ring will release down. Slide the tart from the base onto a large serving platter. The tart can be served warm or at room temperature.

BARDWELL MACARONI AND CHEESE
Makes 8 to 10 servings

....

This recipe is inspired by *American Masala*, by Suvir Saran, a client and neighbor. Suvir has taken mac 'n' cheese to new heights with distinctive herbs and spices. I have adapted it using Consider Bardwell cheeses. It is a standard at any of our farm potluck dinners.

1 pound short pasta (penne, ziti, or elbows)

4 cups grated (about 1 pound) Equinox, or any Italian hard grating cheese

4 cups grated (about 1 pound) Manchester, or a mixture of any soft or semi-hard cheeses

½ cup plain bread crumbs

4 tablespoons (½ stick) unsalted butter

1 teaspoon chopped fresh rosemary

1 teaspoon chopped fresh thyme

1 teaspoon ground peppercorns

1 teaspoon dried red pepper flakes

2 tablespoons all-purpose flour

2 cups milk

1 tablespoon Dijon mustard

1. Preheat the oven to 400°F. Bring a large pot of salted water to a boil, add the pasta, and cook for about 8 minutes, or until not quite al dente. Drain in a colander and set aside.

2. Mix the cheeses together in a large bowl. Transfer ½ cup of

cheese to a small bowl and mix in the bread crumbs to make the topping.

3. In a large pot, melt the butter and add the rosemary, thyme, ground peppercorns, and dried red pepper flakes. Cook over medium-high heat until the mixture is fragrant, stirring occasionally, about 2 minutes. Reduce the heat to medium and whisk in the flour. Continue whisking the flour and herbs for about 1 minute. Drizzle in a couple of tablespoons of milk and whisk to combine. Once the milk is incorporated, whisk in a couple more tablespoons of milk. Repeat until the flour paste is somewhat loose, with no lumps. Whisk in the remaining milk until smooth. Increase the heat to medium-high and cook, stirring, until the sauce thickens slightly, 3 to 4 minutes. Whisk in the mustard and cook another 30 seconds. Add the grated cheeses and stir until melted.

4. Stir the drained pasta into the sauce, then transfer to a 3-quart casserole dish. Sprinkle with the bread crumb–cheese topping and bake until bubbly, about 30 minutes. Serve immediately.

RASPBERRY TART
Makes one 10-inch tart

....

Baking was my secret life! Even though I was running a literary agency, a farm, and a cheese business, I loved baking for the café. My Raspberry Tart was the favorite breakfast at the Fish and Game Café, especially with whipped cream—yes, even at breakfast. It is super simple. When short on time, I would buy a jar of elegant raspberry jam from a specialty store, such as Fauchon in New York City (but you can use your favorite), rather than make my own. Friends liked this tart so much that they would order one to take as a house gift.

THE SWEET PASTRY CRUST

2½ cups all-purpose flour

¼ cup sugar

1 teaspoon salt

1 cup (2 sticks) chilled unsalted butter, cut into small pieces

1 large egg yolk

¼ cup ice water

THE TART

2 pints fresh raspberries

½ cup water

½ cup sugar

1 pint heavy cream, chilled

1. Make the sweet pastry crust: In a food processor, pulse the flour, sugar, and salt until combined. Add the butter and process until the mixture resembles coarse meal, 8 to 10 seconds.

2. In a small bowl, beat together the egg yolk and ice water. With the machine running, pour the egg mixture in a steady stream through the feed tube, processing until the dough just holds together when pinched, 10 to 15 seconds.

3. Divide the dough in half. Flatten each half into a disk; wrap in plastic. Refrigerate the dough at least 1 hour or overnight, or freeze up to 1 month.

4. Make the tart: Preheat the oven to 400°F. Wash the berries and dry each gently.

5. Put one pint of the berries into a small saucepan with the water and sugar. Mash the berries while stirring over medium heat until the jam mixture is thickened and spreadable. Set it aside to cool.

6. Whip the cold heavy cream in the bowl of a mixer using the whipping attachment for about 2 minutes. Set it aside in the refrigerator.

7. Roll out one of the sweet pastry crust dough disks to 10 inches in diameter, then lay it over the rolling pin and transfer it to the tart pan. Fit it into the pan and crimp the edges. Poke holes in the bottom with a fork. (The other half of the dough can be frozen for later use.)

8. Lay aluminum foil over the dough and use pie weights or dried beans to weigh it down. Bake for 10 minutes. Take the crust out of the oven and remove the pie weights and foil. Bake, uncovered, for another 15 minutes, or until golden brown. Let the tart crust cool on a wire rack. To remove the

tart from the pan, gently set it on a large can; the outside ring will release down. Transfer the tart from the base to a decorative plate.

9. Spread the cooled berry jam on the crust. Place the individual berries on top in concentric circles from the inside out. Dress the tart with peaks of whipped cream.

VANILLA BEAN CHEESECAKE

Makes one 6-inch cake; 6 servings

This small no-bake cheesecake is richly delicious and particularly simple because it doesn't have a crust and requires no baking. The vanilla bean imbues it with luscious flavor. For a delightful topper, slice some strawberries or stone fruit, such as peaches or plums, and soak in a bit of sugar and a couple of dashes of rum along with the seeds of the other half of the vanilla bean.

I love this recipe so much that I used to sell this cheescake at the West River Farmers' Market in Londonderry, Vermont. It's from my client Lauren Chattman's book *Instant Gratification* (Morrow). I use Consider Bardwell Farm Mettowee, of course.

2 tablespoons water

½ teaspoon unflavored gelatin

1 vanilla bean

16 ounces Mettowee, any fresh chèvre, or even Philadelphia
   cream cheese

6 tablespoons heavy cream

⅔ cup sugar

1. Place the water in a medium bowl and sprinkle with gelatin. Let stand to dissolve, 2 to 3 minutes. Meanwhile, spray a 6-inch springform pan with cooking spray.

2. Place 1 inch of water in a small saucepan and bring to a bare simmer over medium-low heat. Place the bowl with the gelatin and water on top of the saucepan (it should rest on the edge of the saucepan above the water) and stir just until the gelatin

mixture is smoothly blended, 1 to 2 minutes. Take the bowl off the heat. Do not overheat.

3. Place the vanilla bean on a work surface and split it in half lengthwise using a paring knife. Place one half in plastic wrap and reserve for another use. Scrape the seeds from the other half into a large bowl and add the chèvre, heavy cream, and sugar.

4. Beat with a mixer until light and fluffy, 2 to 3 minutes, scraping down the sides of the bowl once or twice. Beat in the gelatin mixture until well blended.

5. Scrape the cheesecake batter into the pan and smooth the top with a spatula. Cover with plastic wrap and refrigerate until firm, at least 6 hours or overnight.

6. To unmold, run a paring knife around the edge of the pan and gently release the sides of the pan. Set the cake, supported by the springform base, on a cake plate. Store for up to four days in the refrigerator.

acknowledgments

ANGELA MILLER

I am grateful to so many people for helping us get started on the farm and for keeping us on course. They are too numerous to name, and I wouldn't want to accidentally leave anyone out. Just be sure that I do remember you and thank you from the bottom of my heart. A few must be named:

Our partners, Peter Dixon and Chris Gray. Farm and cheese staff past and present, especially Leslie Goff, who has weathered every storm and stuck with us. A generous West Pawlet benefactor, Craig Jordan, whose clean and impeccable design gave us our brand logo.

Inspectors Greg Lockwood and Steven Nicholson for keeping us out of trouble. Sally Eugair of the United States Department of Agriculture. Phyllis Torrey, Diane Heleba, and Marge Christy at the Vermont Agency of Agriculture.

Our farming neighbors who have helped us out of so many

binds: the Clevelands, the Collards, the Hosleys, the Huletts, the Lewises, and Jim Stearns. Thanks to Monty and Sarah Post for so many kindnesses. Laura Brown, Chris Gray's weekend Cheese Widow who takes flashy pictures of the farm, works the markets, and supports us in so many ways. Lisa Kaiman and Karen Guttman, who produce the most wonderful milk. The West Pawlet Fire Department for keeping us safe. The Granville Veterinary Service for keeping our herd healthy. The farmers' markets of Vermont and New York City for allowing us to reach out to local customers every week.

The amazing cheese and specialty shops that carry our cheeses, with special thanks to Liz Thorpe, Max McCalman, and Anne Saxelby for their support from the get-go. My pals Philippa Katz and Judy Lake for long walks and girls' nights out; and Judy and Jay Inglis, who started it all by inviting us to their Thanksgiving dinner in 2000, and Julie Doetsch and Debbie Gardner for being friends forever. Without Debbie there would never have been a book.

My partners at the Miller Agency, Sharon Bowers and Jennifer Griffin, who are brilliant and cover for me in so many ways—and who are responsible for getting this book off the ground—as well as my steadfast clients who write the most amazing books. A special hug to Mark Bittman, who is such a good friend. I also thank Mark Bittman, Jean-Georges Vongerichten, Suvir Saran, Lauren Chattman, and the team of Frank Mentesana and Jerome Audureau with Carolynn Carreño for letting me share my version of their recipes.

A big thanks to the publishing staff at John Wiley & Sons, especially our editor Linda Ingroia, as well as Natalie Chapman, the publisher, and Rob Garber, the executive publisher. I also appreciate the special efforts of Ava Wilder, the dedicated production editor; Jeff Faust, the cover designer; Rebecca Scherm, the editorial assistant and illustrator; Debbie Glasserman, the interior designer; and Francesco Tonelli, the photographer. Thanks to Todd Fries and Michael Friedberg in marketing and David Greenberg in publicity for promoting my book.

Above all, I thank my husband, Russell Glover; my daughter, Samantha Skolnik; my sister, Cynthia Taylor; and my brother, Dan Miller; as well as my herd of Oberhasli dairy goats, whose big personalities first captured my heart on that August day in 2003 when we crossed the Green Mountains together.

And to my coauthor, Ralph Gardner Jr., for helping me put my experiences on paper and for putting up with my distractions, postponements, and excuses. I cannot express enough thanks for your being so gracious for nearly two years.

RALPH GARDNER JR.

Consider Bardwell's employees—Margot Brooks, Alex Eaton, Bob Hahn, Minny Buley, Leslie Goff, Amber Goff, Laura Fletcher, Corey Chapin, and Sue Olsen—answered my questions about everything from milking goats to their personal lives with good cheer.

Peter Dixon was immeasurably patient in explaining the mysteries of cheese making and aging—not once, but several times, and then correcting the manuscript himself when I still didn't get it. Chris Gray let me bug him while he was trying to serve customers at farmers' markets, but his talents as a salesman are such that I don't believe he lost a single sale.

Any story is in the details, and Linda Ingroia, our editor, demanded a lot more of them, markedly improving the manuscript.

I thank my wife Debbie for her love and friendship, and for reading the manuscript more than once. Most of all, I want to thank my friend Angela Miller, whose energy and ambition remain only slightly less inscrutable to me, and her accomplishments even more impressive, than when we embarked on *Hay Fever* almost two years ago.

index

W

washed rind, 93–94, 101, 177. *See also* Dorset cheese; Manchester cheese; Pawlet cheese

Weinberg, Karen, 6

West Pawlet Fish and Game Café, 70–79, 221, 243, 266, 271

West Pawlet Fish and Game Club, 72–73, 74

West Pawlet Quarry, 22, 178. *See also* Chester cheese

Y

Yoko (goat), 163

Z

Zabar's, 19

Zena (goat), 36, 42, 85, 94

Zingerman's, 173–174, 176, 180, 186

Zoe (goat), 240